To the Ronnies

[signature]

Tim Wilkin

THE DISTRIBUTION TRAP

Also by Andrew R. Thomas

Direct Marketing in Action: Cutting-Edge Strategies for Finding and Keeping the Best Customers (with Dale M. Lewison, William J. Hauser, and Linda M. Foley)

Defining the Really Great Boss (with M. David Dealy)

Global Manifest Destiny: Growing Your Business in a Borderless Economy (with John Caslione)

Aviation Insecurity: The New Challenges of Air Travel

Managing by Accountability: What Every Leader Needs to Know About Responsibility, Integrity . . . and Results (with M. David Dealy)

The Rise of Women Entrepreneurs: People, Processes, and Global Trends (with Jeanne Halladay Coughlin)

Supply Chain Security: International Practices and Innovations in Moving Goods Safely and Efficiently

Growing Your Business in Emerging Markets: Promise and Perils (with John Caslione)

Aviation Security Management (3 vols.)

Air Rage: Crisis in the Skies

Change or Die! How to Transform Your Organization from the Inside Out (with M. David Dealy)

The Handbook of Supply Chain Security

The Greatest Thing Ever Built: The Saturn V Spaceship (with Paul Thomarios)

Also by Thomas J. Wilkinson

The New World Marketing, vol. 3 of *Marketing in the 21st Century*

THE DISTRIBUTION TRAP

Keeping Your Innovations from Becoming Commodities

Andrew R. Thomas and Timothy J. Wilkinson

PRAEGER
An Imprint of ABC-CLIO, LLC

A B C ☰ C L I O

Santa Barbara, California • Denver, Colorado • Oxford, England

Library of Congress Cataloging-in-Publication Data

Thomas, Andrew R.
  The distribution trap : keeping your innovations from becoming commodities / Andrew R. Thomas, Timothy J. Wilkinson.
    p. cm.
  Includes bibliographical references and index.
  ISBN 978-0-313-36552-2 (hbk.: alk. paper)—ISBN 978-0-313-36553-9 (ebook)
  1. Distributors (Commerce) 2. Dealers (Retail trade) 3. New products—Marketing. I. Wilkinson, Timothy J. II. Title.
  HF5422.T56 2010
  658.8'7—dc22   2009035110

ISBN: 978-0-313-36552-2
EISBN: 978-0-313-36553-9

14 13 12 11 10   1 2 3 4 5

This book is also available on the World Wide Web as an eBook.
Visit www.abc-clio.com for details.

Praeger
An Imprint of ABC-CLIO, LLC

ABC-CLIO, LLC
130 Cremona Drive, P.O. Box 1911
Santa Barbara, California 93116-1911

This book is printed on acid-free paper ∞

Manufactured in the United States of America

CONTENTS

PREFACE

The American business model is dysfunctional. Small to medium-size companies, the backbone of U.S. capitalism, have been drawn into a misconceived form of marketing and selling. It works like this: Companies invest blood sweat, tears, and money to innovate a product; sell it through the largest distributor possible; maximize the volume of sales through that distributor; deal with the inevitable cost-cutting demands; export capital, jobs, quality control, and pollution to developing markets; watch the innovation become a commodity; lose money; begin to develop a new innovation; and then start all over again.

Much of what has driven us into the Great Recession is rooted here. Sell more and more through a Mega-distributor—with much of the profits split by distributors and overseas manufacturers. Earnings obtained by the latter are reinvested into the United States and then are lent to consumers so they can buy more and more. The cycle is repeated. Discussions are abundant about out-of-control lending and consumer spending, the impact of more outsourcing, and the lack of sustainability; but little attention is paid to the role of sales and distribution strategy and its harmful effect on businesses and the economy in general.

As we talk to business leaders around the world, it is clear that many of them realize a fundamental shift has occurred: Power is transferring from those who create innovative products and services to Mega-distributors, who are controlling more and more of the global marketplace. Mistakenly, many companies see deals with Mega-distributors as *the* way to boost sales and market share.

In reality, the Megas, as we call them, live by high volume and low prices. The Megas use their powerful leverage to demand price cuts and other concessions from their suppliers. Companies end up with thin profit margins, and their innovative products and services are often treated as little more than commodities.

Surprisingly, this transformation of the business landscape has occurred with little fanfare or real analysis. Under the banner of "core competencies"—that is, where companies are told to focus on the few things they are really good at and outsource the rest—the critical functions of sales and distribution are too often left to others. Hardly anyone has noticed what is happening. For many companies, it is too late.

Part I

Setting Up for Failure

Thomas Edison could have been talking about the Distribution Trap when he observed that "[m]any of life's failures are people who did not realize how close they were to success when they gave up." For companies who pour all they have into innovating great products, services, and brands, nothing is more depressing than watching them fail when it comes to the critical next step. Still, falling into the Distribution Trap is not something that just happens.

Chapter 1

THE DISTRIBUTION TRAP

When you find yourself in the majority, pause and reflect.
—Mark Twain

When we talk to the people who lead companies—from huge multi-nationals to one-person start-ups—a lot of them think that if they could just get their product or service into the hands of the Mega-distributor that dominates their industry, somehow all of their problems would go away.

Most of us have heard the business adage that "volume covers all sins." If we can just make enough sales, profits will rise, business with grow, and we will be more successful than we ever could have imagined.

One of the most influential of all developments in business over the past four decades has been the rise of large-scale retailers—what we call the Mega-distributors, or Megas for short. You know who we are talking about—Wal-Mart, The Home Depot, Lowe's, Best Buy, and the other huge big-box stores. In the case of automobiles, Mega-distributors like AutoNation dominate sales. In the insurance business, large agents or brokers who represent multiple lines of insurance products control which offerings actually end up in front of prospective buyers. In financial services, companies that underwrite products, from auto financing to student loans, give an incredible number of incentives and discounts to those firms that actually deal with the end user.

For many companies, the "dreams of glory" that stem from partnering with a Mega are simply irresistible. Benefits such as exposure to hundreds of millions of potential customers and the ability to streamline account management—to have only a few customers instead of hundreds or thousands—are quite attractive. Sales volumes grow logarithmically and new national brands can appear practically overnight.

But behind these high hopes, there is a faulty premise, and it is one that has led to disaster for many companies. Whether it is out of naïveté, arrogance, or greed, companies that create innovative products and services expect that Megas will care about the success of their innovations as much as they do. The Megas do not. They never have and never will.

What innovative companies do not know, what they forget, or what they ignore is that the business model Mega-distributors leverage to has a tremendous advantage. Mega-distributors wield their unbridled power to dictate terms to their suppliers. Because of their supremacy, Megas ultimately insist on greater price reductions and force companies to redesign the products or services they deliver to better suit their needs. In the end, what many companies discover is that all the blood, sweat, tears, money, and effort that was poured into developing an innovation has simply been wasted. Dishearteningly, their hard-won creations have been turned into commodities with razor-thin or nonexistent profit margins. This is "profitless prosperity" in action.

Megas not only insist that vendors reduce prices, but also get "under the hood" by forcing producers to engage in a variety of activities that the Megas deem to be financially advantageous. These activities to offload include the following:

- Shifting bulk-breaking responsibilities to manufacturers
- Forcing manufacturers to deliver directly to stores, not to distribution centers owned by the Megas
- Requiring producers to deliver pallets that contain items for specific departments within a store
- Making manufacturers ship smaller case packs so that full cases can be placed on the store shelf
- Paying suppliers only after the product is sold at retail
- Requiring vendors to use new inventory management technologies
- Insisting that manufacturers redesign their entire supply chains

A study published in 1997 that examined the items outlined above found that these practices, for the most part, were initiated by the Megas rather than producers. Moreover, the changes were perceived to be required, not voluntary.[1]

The lure of what we call the "Distribution Trap" is the promise of incredible wealth. Everyone who gets a product accepted by Wal-Mart becomes wealthy, right? The trap is sprung when Levi's, Rubbermaid, Goodyear, or mom-and-pop innovators make the trip to Bentonville, Arkansas (Wal-Mart's headquarters), and sign on the dotted line. The Distribution Trap is signing over control of the sales and distribution of your innovations to the Mega. Once done, the amount of time it takes for your hard-won innovations to become commodities is accelerated. And, because of huge pressure from the Mega for deep price reductions, high-cost domestic operations are shuttered, and it becomes necessary to chase the cheapest labor around the world. To make matters worse, once in the Distribution Trap, it is almost impossible to get out—unless the "out" is "out of business."

BUT IT'S NOT WAL-MART'S FAULT!

Before we go any further, and you begin to think this is merely another book written to point the finger at Wal-Mart and others for the ills of the world, let us be clear: We do not blame the Megas for the Distribution Trap and what it leads to. A trap can exist only if someone is willing to take the bait. There seem to be a lot of willing victims.

We believe that the true responsibility for a company's innovative products and services lies with that same company. Nobody at Wal-Mart's headquarters in Bentonville, Arkansas, forces a potential supplier to come knocking on his or her door. In fact, Wal-Mart and most other Megas do not travel to potential suppliers. They wait for potential suppliers to come to them. And, boy, do these manufacturers show up—in great numbers, each hoping to strike it rich.

The Megas are merely by-products of a contagion that has spread across American business and is now being exported to the rest of the world. Beginning in the early 1980s, the United States began to see a push in which innovative firms permitted, either consciously or subconsciously, outsiders into their companies. They allowed these outsiders to control more and more of their sales and distribution activities. Innovative companies and the people who led them were responding to what management theorists were saying at that time. The "business gurus" talked about organizational transformation—emphasizing things like resources, capabilities, innovation, technology, and operational effectiveness. Terms like "total quality management," "lean manufacturing," and "zero defects" were just some of the solutions being preached by the business elites to companies of all sizes.

Central to transformation was the idea of outsourcing. It was held that the leaders of an organization needed to identify those areas where they excelled—where they brought true value to the marketplace—and effectively outsource the rest. Drinking this elixir, thousands of companies that once had been in control of all aspects of their innovative development began to lose interest in sales and distribution, preferring instead that other companies take over this "business function." The concept of "core competencies," which is still a mainstay of management education, was provided as the justification for letting control loose after the producing firm had exercised its unique set of value-adding activities. Why manage a string of dealers if your core competency—your basis of differentiation—is in research and development (R&D) or manufacturing? Taking this advice, companies divested themselves of activities that were not perceived as value added, and they pushed sales and distribution aside.

One of the people who understood the new Harvard thinking better than anyone was Sam Walton. He and a raft of imitators stepped in to fill the power vacuum that the strategy gurus had helped to create. The result was the evolution of massive distributors, which ultimately drove the sales and distribution of innovative products and services in the United States.

In the 21st century, most consumer products and services are sold, distributed, and controlled by entities other than the ones that actually created those products and services. In a country where more than 70 percent of the economy depends on consumer spending, we find that, overwhelmingly, the ability of companies to take their innovative products and services and get them into the hands of consumers is blocked, thwarted, or controlled by Mega-distributors. Thousands, literally tens of thousands, of innovative companies have little or no control over the distribution and sale of their products or services. They do not even have control over the prices that they can charge for those innovations. This is evidenced by mandates from Mega-distributors who, year after year, impose price reductions on these innovations while insisting that their suppliers maintain high standards of quality and service.

The ability of Wal-Mart to squeeze its suppliers is legendary. This is because it dominates an estimated 30 percent of the U.S. market for all household staples—things like toothpaste, shampoo, and paper products. It is the biggest seller of CDs, DVDs, and books in the country. This company's vendors have no choice but to toe the line, and, as a result, the power Wal-Mart wields means that the innovative company who is selling to them is getting further and further away from the end user who is actually consuming the product or service.

SO WHAT IS A MEGA?

Category killers, discounters, and mass merchandisers are contemporary terms for what we refer to as the Mega-distributor. On the retail side, Megas can be subdivided into four categories: discount department stores, outlet stores, warehouse clubs, and category killers.

Discount Department Stores

These discount department stores range in size from 80,000 to 130,000 square feet, and they offer a wide range of merchandise, including home furnishings, housewares, automotive parts and services, cosmetics, and clothing. Prominent discount department stores include Wal-Mart, Target, and Kmart.

Outlet Stores

Typically, outlets stores are discount operations of major department stores like JCPenny and Nordstrom, as well as manufacturers such as G.H. Bass, Burlington Coat Factory, and Nike. Square footage ranges from 20,000 to 80,000 square feet.

Warehouse Clubs

Ranging from 104,000 to 170,000 square feet, warehouse clubs are the giants of the giants. Generally, warehouse clubs offer only a limited number of product items (5,000 or less), which are sold in bulk, but they offset the limited selection with wholesale prices. Examples include Costco, Sam's Club, Pace Membership Warehouse, and BJ's Wholesale Club.

Category Killers

Category killers offer a large selection of products in a single category. Ranging from 20,000 to 120,000 square feet, these Megas include Sports Authority, Lowe's, The Home Depot, Best Buy, and Toys"R"Us. These stores are designed to dominate the category and kill the competition.

Not all Megas are big-box stores. We include smaller stores, like drug stores (for example, CVS, Rite Aid), along with convenience stores (for example, 7-Eleven, Sheetz), as well as unique entities like automobile dealerships. The point is not the store's format so much as it is the approach of the distributor to the marketplace. In our opinion, distributors that can dominate innovative companies based on their ability to generate volume sales are, by definition, Megas.

In his book *Category Killers*, Robert Spector explains how the Megas interact with the market.

> Category killers . . . have helped expand and upscale the "mass market" by aggressively driving down the prices of goods and services, and making affordable what were once upscale products such as laptop computers, big-screen TVs, or designer apparel. Today, virtually every one of us—regardless of income—is part of the ever-expanding mass market where the differences among stores—Dollar Stores to Kmart to Macy's—are measured in slight gradations. A discount store like Target, which employs its own in-house designers, has made even fashion merchandise just another affordable commodity. (Wal-Mart is now trying to do the same.) Consequently, loyalty to a particular store has become a casualty of our changing consumer culture. At one time, shoppers used to identify with a store, just as they identified with the make of the cars they drove. Today, many of us simply want more and better goods, and we will shop the retailer that provides those goods at a price that we consider "affordable."[2]

As shoppers, we love the discounts offered by the Megas. Buying at the big-box stores does save money—especially when comparison shopping is studiously employed. The better the deal, however, the greater the awareness that something is wrong about the transaction taking place. Everyone knows that there is something untenable about a gallon jar of pickles priced at $2.97. Salmon sold for under $5 a pound is unreal—Kafkaesque even. Although great "deals" abound at the Megas, the city centers of small towns, which at one time had stores selling the full range of merchandise, are now filled with tattoo parlors, head shops, picture framing boutiques, and other "niche" businesses. In the meantime, the neighborhood's retirees are serving as greeters and cashiers at the behemoth retailers. (Do they do this for fun?) All the while, innovative companies vie for the opportunity to sell through the mass-market retailers—the promise of riches beyond measure is too difficult to resist.

WHO IS RESPONSIBLE FOR THE TRAP?

The responsibility and, ultimately, the accountability for the rise of the Megas sits squarely on the shoulders of those executives who decided to outsource their sales and distribution to the Megas in the first place. It was their call and their decision. In looking at the Distribution Trap, it is critical to understand that, when we talk about responsibility and accountability, ultimately it is individual people who must be held to account, not intangible things like corporations. For every important responsibility, like a sales and distribution strategy, there is accountability. Accountability is the obligation to answer for the discharge of responsibilities that affect others. Accountability includes answering for intentions as well as results. Whenever someone has an important responsibility, they have an obligation to answer to stakeholders for their decisions. What we find far too often is that executives, who at one time bought into the temptation of doing business with a Mega and now have realized that they are caught in the Distribution Trap, engage in the blame game. They say things like, "Well, we didn't know that this was going to happen to us." Or "We didn't think that this was going to be the end result."

But, like your parents used to say, you are defined by those you associate with. If an individual decides to travel to Bentonville, sit across the table from Wal-Mart executives, and allow the Mega to become his customer, then he has to realize the potential ramifications of that decision, even before he boards the plane for northwestern Arkansas.

Megas exist. They do not lie about who they are. But, they are not the only option. It is only when companies decide to do business with Megas that the Distribution Trap becomes a reality.

WHAT THIS BOOK IS ABOUT

The subtitle of the book is "Keeping Your Innovations from Becoming Commodities." Our focus is on companies whose primary goal is innovation and the maintenance of these innovations in the marketplace. If you are in the commodity business, this book is not for you—unless you want to get out of the trap in which you may find yourself. We examine the ways in which a company can preserve the value of its innovations and avoid the Distribution Trap. The benefits of doing so can be immense—from higher profits and better sales to keeping jobs in the United States and retaining greater control of your destiny and having more fun at work every day.

The chapters in Part I explore how the dreams of grandeur that fester in the minds of so many leaders, who believe in simply creating an innovation and letting a Mega-distributor handle it, can be nightmares in the making. The consequences often are disastrous.

First, as we will see, selling through the Megas takes the innovative company further and further away from its customers. The ability to service or respond to the needs of buyers disappears when a Mega has entered the mix and is controlling the sales and distribution process. We will look at how both the venerable Goodyear Tire and Rubber Company and Levi Strauss confused their customers with their competitors, to their great detriment.

Second, a breakdown occurs when innovations are commoditized too rapidly. In the natural course of events, today's innovation may very well become a commodity. The Sony Walkman, the IBM Selectric Typewriter, the Macintosh computer, and scores of other technological breakthroughs spent a good bit of time as commodities before becoming obsolete. The product life cycle, while guaranteeing this downward trajectory, does not assign a timetable to the decline of an innovation. The Megas, on the other hand, compress the product life cycle by displaying real innovations next to row upon row of mature products that are already on their way out. Guilt by association works in the retail environment just as it does in a criminal conspiracy. We will explore how both the automotive industry in the United States and Rubbermaid Corporation accelerated the commoditization of their innovations by abrogating control to the Megas in their industries.

If commoditization is viewed as a problem by manufacturers, even greater attempts at innovation is seen as the solution. As firms attempt to increase competitiveness with new products, features, or product extensions, the Mega insists that producing firms meet its price points. As a result, innovators are compelled to outsource the manufacturing of their products to companies operating overseas. This is the third breakdown. It is our view that much of the outsourcing of jobs that has taken place in the United States has not simply been due to companies attempting to lower costs because they are greedy, but because they are forced to reduce expenses to meet the demands of the Megas while still eking out a small profit. Year after year, prices have to go down. In an environment in which globalization has opened up new markets for production, as well as for sales, companies come to a point at which they actually have no other option, if they have fallen into the Distribution Trap, except to close more costly domestic operations and outsource to less expensive international locations.

In the 1990s, the North American Free Trade Agreement (NAFTA) introduced many companies to the advantages of low-cost outsourcing. With China's ascension into the World Trade Organization in 2001, the outsourcing focus shifted. Under the rhetoric of "globalization" and "a billion new customers," companies transferred production to the Middle Kingdom to keep the Megas happy. Now, even China is becoming too expensive. Companies are moving manufacturing to Vietnam and Bangladesh, and services are moving to low-cost environments like India and the Philippines. The outsourcing compulsion—the reality that a firm must offshore production to stay in business—is being driven by the Distribution Trap.

Having come this far in the chapter, you may have the impression that there is no hope—that if you want to create a product that is well known and readily available to consumers, you simply must do business with the Megas. This is decidedly not the case. It is possible for a start-up, a medium-size firm, or even a large company to stay clear of the Distribution Trap. Part II of this book explores how to do just that. It will concentrate on the following:

- How to control sales and distribution channels from the very beginning, from the origins of the innovation until they are purchased by the end user
- How direct marketing, which we believe to be the best and most successful way of doing marketing, offers low costs and incredibly high rewards for companies that choose not to be tempted by the Distribution Trap
- How, in an increasingly global world, it is possible to go global without having to engage the Mega-distributors overseas

The spotlight will be on profitability—not on the mistaken belief that volume covers all sins. A successful company may not be the biggest in its industry, sell the most products, deliver the most services, or have the biggest top-line sales at the end of the year. But so what?

If a business stays out of the Distribution Trap, it can more easily maximize the value of its innovations, control quality, and enhance relationships with its best customers. It also will not be forced to offshore and outsource because of the demands of Wal-Mart, The Home Depot, or Lowe's.

Ultimately, we believe that avoiding the Distribution Trap is the best way to build a real, sustainable enterprise today and for the future—that with all the discussion about the decline of American ingenuity, scarcity of resources, global competition, uncertainty about economic future, and doubts about the role of government, controlling sales and distribution is the cornerstone of business success—as it always has been.

NOTES

1. Christopher D. Norek, "Mass Merchant Discounters: Drivers of Logistics Change," *Journal of Business Logistics*, 18, no. 1 (1997): 1–17.
2. Robert Spector, *Category Killers: The Retail Revolution and Its Impact on Consumer Culture* (Cambridge, MA: Harvard Business School Press, 2005), p. 29.

Chapter 2

THE (D)EVOLUTION
OF DISTRIBUTION

History is a grand gallery, with many copies and only a few
originals.

—Alexis De Tocqueville

The story of the forerunners of today's Megas shows that the current dominance of the mass discounters is less about the birth of
something new than it is about the mutation of something old.
Long before the present-day mass marketers began to call the
shots, a long line of peddlers, shop owners, wholesalers, and various kinds of mass merchandisers displaced each other, even as
changes took place in manufacturing, infrastructure development,
and competition.

THE 19TH CENTURY

In the middle of the 19th century, distribution was a haphazard
proposition. As the United States spread westward, settlers were
served by itinerant peddlers who sold items obtained from eastern
cities or from isolated western outposts. Shopkeepers in remote
areas filled their inventories through semiannual shopping trips
to large cities. The development of the railroad and the telegraph,
innovations that make today's Internet pale by comparison, trans-
formed all business enterprises by the end of the century into the
structures familiar to us today.

The initial beneficiary of the new technologies consisted of wholesalers, also known as "jobbers." These individuals took titles to goods purchased directly from producers through big buying networks and sold to general stores on the frontier through—at that time—large-scale marketing organizations. The speed and predictability of the railroad, coupled with the ability to order goods through the telegraph, expanded the distribution capacity of jobbers, thereby reducing unit costs, which in turn led to higher profits. Just as the convenience of the new system allowed shopkeepers to concentrate on their local businesses, manufacturers benefited by receiving immediate payment rather than having to wait for their goods to be sold.

With the end of the Civil War, the country store of the Midwest spread throughout the South, supplied by full-service wholesaling firms that dominated distribution during the second half of the century. Supported by a legion of salesmen that traveled by train and carriage, wholesalers were able to help shopkeepers upgrade operations, improve accounting practices, and enhance merchandise presentation. In addition, they developed sophisticated purchasing operations. The activity of these buyers varied greatly because each product line required specific expertise and a specialized approach to the market.

In some instances, goods were sourced directly from manufacturers overseas. Circumstances sometimes required that private brands be developed for the wholesalers. At other moments, a wholesaler would become the sole distributor for a manufacturer's product. While backward integration into manufacturing occurred on occasion, most wholesalers focused on buying and selling rather than producing.

The wholesaler was largely an organizer of economic activity. Functional areas typically included the "traffic" department, which dealt with scheduling shipments from manufacturers, to warehouses, to retailers. As the system developed, a measure of performance evolved that is still with us today. Stock-turn was defined as "the number of times stock on hand was sold and replaced within a specified time period, usually annually."[1] Stock-turn measured the velocity of distribution. High stock-turn meant that products were spending less time sitting on storeroom shelves, which meant lower unit costs and higher output per worker. The development of the telegraph and the railroad made a high stock-turn an achievable objective and created the possibility of mass marketing.

THE EMERGENCE OF MASS RETAILING

By 1880, wholesalers began to be surpassed by either mass retailers, who bought directly from producers and sold through their own stores, or by manufacturers who built their own wholesale operations. In both instances, the activities of the previously dominant wholesalers were taken over, creating greater operational efficiencies. Retailers prevailed because they were able to achieve greater economies of scale (lower costs associated with the higher volume of a product) and scope (lower costs associated with the marketing of different types of products) than wholesalers.

The new mass retailers came in four forms: department stores, mail-order houses, retail chains, and vertically integrated firms.

Department Stores

Department stores were an urban phenomenon. Retail operations that sold clothing or dry goods became department stores when they added furniture, glassware, jewelry, and other new product lines. Macy's and Bloomingdale's followed this course as did Nieman Marcus and Marshall Field. The impetus behind the department store was the burgeoning of city populations in the decades following the Civil War. As the cities swelled with people, new lines were added—carpets, upholstered goods, furs, men's and women's clothing, hats, shoes, and toys—to satisfy the demands of a new, urban consumer class. The strategy of these stores was fairly uniform:

> They were aimed at maintaining the high volume, high turnover flow of business by selling at low prices and low margins. Profits were to be made on volume, not markup. . . . Above all, the mass retailers concentrated on maintaining a high level of stock-turn. This they did by marking down slow-moving lines, by extensive local advertising, and by creating a clearly defined management structure.[2]

The department stores were managed as decentralized holding companies. The department head was king, free to make nearly all decisions about buying and selling goods, accountable to the central organization only for his financial performance.

The head of a shoe department, for example, would make all of the decisions about where to buy shoes, how to price shoes, and even how advertising copy would read in the store's shoe ads.

Occasionally, department stores would integrate backward into manufacturing to produce a limited selection of products like clothing or upholstery. This was fairly rare, and, in any case, management avoided controlling or managing the activities of their suppliers. Instead, as mentioned earlier, the strategy of the early departments was based on stock-turn (velocity). For example, Marshall Field had a stock-turn of five for most of the 20th century, while Macy's had a stock-turn of twelve for the year 1887. High stock-turns led to the ability to make more money with lower margins by selling at lower prices. Small retailers, complaining bitterly about this new, unfair competition, demanded state legislation that would protect them from the lower prices of the department stores.

Mail-Order Houses

The telegraph and railroad paved the way for the first direct marketers. Though present in a limited form before the Civil War, mail-order houses came into full bloom in the years that followed. The first organization to sell a wide variety of products exclusively through catalog sales was Montgomery Ward, with catalogs in excess of 500 pages listing about 24,000 products. Sears and Roebuck followed and, by 1895, sold practically every consumer product that was then available through a 532-page catalog. Items included shoes, wagons, fishing tackle, stoves, china, saddles, firearms, buggies, glassware, and musical instruments. Sales of $400,000 in 1893 nearly doubled two years later.[3] Like the department stores of the day, each merchandising department was fully autonomous, where the buyer was in complete control of volume, catalog pricing, and the prices paid to vendors. The geometric growth in sales volume experienced by the mail-order houses prompted them to integrate backward into manufacturing. By 1906, Sears operated sixteen manufacturing plants to maintain a steady supply of items for its numerous product lines. Its sophisticated system of logistics allowed it to surpass the retail volume of the department stores.

The ability of Sears and Montgomery Ward to increase profits through lower prices based on velocity (high stock-turn) and lower margins, created a political fracas during the first decade of the 20th century. Smaller retailers and wholesalers railed against perceived unfair competition just as they had against department stores during previous decades. Despite protests, a bill extending parcel post service into rural areas was passed in 1912. Mass retailing was not stymied by entrenched, local interests. In fact, it was fostered by government action.

Chain Stores

Chain stores came to the fore of American retailing at the beginning of the new century. By the 1920s, they were under the same sort of political attack that had landed on the department stores and mail-order houses years before. Chain stores differed from department stores in two ways: First, they consisted of multiple stores carrying similar merchandise spread out over a geographic area. Second, unlike the department stores and mail-order houses, they were centrally managed. Where buyers in the other forms of retail enterprise operated departments as independent principalities, managers of chain stores took their orders from the central office.

Referring to chain stores, one writer from the 1920s stated, "Some are centrally owned but independently operated. Some are centrally controlled and operated—this being the prevailing and most successful type."[4] The key was standardization. Buyers consisted of specialists at the chain's headquarters. Hiring and firing was controlled by personnel departments. Store managers were likened to engineers operating locomotives:

> The process of standardization is extended to almost every phase of chain activity; the stores are alike in appearance; the interior equipment is the same; the stock and position of the stock on the shelves of one store corresponds to that of any other store in the chain; the instructions given for running the stores are identical. Each manager has to fill out the same forms daily; to carry out the same routine of caring for cash, of locking up for the night, of all the detailed minutiae of storekeeping.[5]

The first chain stores focused on groceries, followed by variety stores. Woolworths operated seven stores in Pennsylvania in the early 1880s. By the turn of the century, it had sales of $5 million, and by 1909, it operated 318 stores throughout the United States. As with the other retailers, stock-turn was the criterion upon which success was based. In the mid-1920s, Sears and Montgomery Ward began chain stores of their own; a similar course was followed by large department stores in the 1930s.

During this period, producer-retailer relationships were under stress largely due to the power exercised by manufacturers coupled with the lack of interdependency among production and distribution activities. For most of the century, communications were carried out through the mail or through expensive long-distance phone calls. Computers, which did not become commercially available until the 1960s, were expensive, difficult to use, and did not communicate with each other. Industry leader Wal-Mart did not begin using information technology to coordinate with its vendors until 1987, and e-mail was not widely used until the mid-1990s. The ability to communicate, which we take for granted today, was a more complicated undertaking in years past.

Vertically Integrated Firms

During the 20th century, the exception to the middleman situation existed in the vertically integrated firm, which combined manufacturing along with the sales and distribution function. By coordinating business activities within the firm rather than through external markets, producing companies could control all aspects of distribution, avoid dealing with intermediaries, and eliminate the need to negotiate with sales entities. Manufacturers developed distribution capacity, including sales, service, financing, installation, and other appropriate ancillary activities. By owning their own retail outlets, these firms were able to monitor customer desires, better understand markets, and more carefully plan how best to approach buyer segments. National Cash Register, Remington Typewriter, Eastman Kodak, and Pabst Brewing Co. are examples of producers that operated their own retail outlets during this period.

EMERGENCE OF THE MEGAS

Although telecommunications, rails, and eventually trucking provided the means through which mass distribution expanded during the 20th century, relationships between producers and end users were limited. Transactions were overwhelmingly at arm's length, wherein manufacturers exploited economies of scale to lower costs, maximize production, and "push" their products onto the marketplace with little understanding of how much consumer demand really existed.

The need to coordinate supply and demand was filled by wholesalers, dealers, and distributors—middlemen—that stood between manufacturers and retailers. By managing huge inventories, these intermediaries served as buffers between producers and sellers, thereby limiting the need for coordination between the two.[6] Later, technological advances created new tools that changed the dynamics between manufacturers and consumers.

The great business historian Alfred Chandler explained the underlying economic logic of the wholesalers and new mass-market retailers, along with the emergence of the Megas:

> The intermediaries' cost advantage had resulted from exploiting the economies of both scale and scope. Because they handled the products of many manufacturers, they achieved a greater volume and lower costs per unit than did any one manufacturer in the marketing and distribution of a *single* line of products (scale). Moreover, they increased this advantage by the broader scope of their operation— that is, by handling a number of related product lines through a single set of activities (scope).[7]

Velocity was king. Economies of scale and scope ruled. What Chandler labeled as "managerial capitalism" was based on the idea that managers coordinated production and distribution activities within huge firms because it was more efficient than allowing the market to handle transactions through the "invisible hand." In fact, Chandler titled one of his books on the topic the *Visible Hand*, implying that the invisible hand of the marketplace had been displaced by the visible hand of managerial activity. He stated that "[t]he mass marketers replaced merchants as distributors of goods in the American economy because they internalized a high volume of market transactions within a single large modern enterprise."[8]

Increasing stock-turn by growing volume, adding new lines of products, and opening new outlets allowed the mass marketers to price their products below that of smaller retailers who relied on wholesalers and to still be more profitable than those wholesalers. The mass-market retailers who benefited from this process—Gimbels, Hartfords, Woolworths, Kresge's, and others—became phenomenally wealthy.

Beginning in the late 1970s, technological advances accelerated the amount of inefficiency that could be squeezed out of the retail sector. Today, it is difficult to imagine a time when checkers manually entered numbers into a cash register and counted back change correctly, or when an individual standing in line waited patiently while the person in front of him slowly wrote out a check. Supply chain management, data mining, and analytics, along with sophisticated logistics and inventory controls, led to the rise of the Megas.

The big change came in 1987, heralded by a new approach that came out of the relationship between Proctor & Gamble (P&G) and Wal-Mart. A former Wal-Mart executive explained what happened:

> [W]e both decided that the entire relationship between vendor and retailer was at issue. Both had focused on the end-user—the customer—but each did it independently of the other. No sharing of information, no planning together, no systems coordination. We were simply two giant entities going our separate ways, oblivious to the excess costs created by the obsolete system. We were communicating, in effect, by slipping notes under the door. . . . Following the P&G/Wal-Mart partnership, many other companies began to view the supplier as an important partner.[9]

Improvements in manufacturing processes and technology were making it possible for suppliers to the new Megas to customize products according to the requirements of the end user. The need for extensive inventories diminished as the "marketing concept" became widespread, and producers developed the capability to tailor-make products with short production runs through just-in-time manufacturing and other methods.

THE CURRENT SYSTEM

Businesses in distribution networks are now dependent on the products and services offered by other firms. Increasing populations and incomes, highly competitive environments, globalization, specialization, a focus on core competencies, and the ability to "unbundle" the value-adding activities of the firms involved in producing and distributing products has created an environment in which the "invisible hand" of the market seems to rule once again.

In many respects, the structure of this new model looks more like that of the antebellum era than like that of the era of managerial capitalism. Production takes place in numerous distinct firms, whose outputs are coordinated through market exchange broadly understood. . . . Vertical disintegration and specialization is perhaps the most significant organizational development of the late 20th century.[10]

The difference between then and now is that, rather than being led by the producers, the Mega-distributors are clearly in the driver's seat. The Megas dominate the business landscape— not just the retail environment—for five major reasons: low price, inventory management, outsourcing, the commoditization of products, and the advent of private-label goods. Through disciplined execution in each of these areas, they have pushed less motivated retailers to the side and have forced manufacturers to fall into line.

Low Price

Everyone who grew up in the 1960s or before can remember conversations in which people bragged about how much they paid for something. To have paid more for a product indicated that a higher-quality item had been purchased. Not so today. For the last thirty years, bragging rights have gone to the person who got a good price, a fabulous discount, a great deal. Pricing is, by definition, relative. The most influential factor that shapes pricing is competition. Consumer price sensitivity—resulting from discounting, sales, or everyday low prices—has become the norm in the American business environment.

As prices are lowered, competitors must respond to low prices, which, in turn, encourages consumers to shop for what they perceive to be bargains. With the advent of greater price transparency through the Internet, price-based competition has only increased. A study by UBS Warburg found that Wal-Mart's prices are, on average, 14 percent below that of the competition. Wal-Mart is so big that it has the ability to lower the price on any items that it wants reduced for any reason. It often cites findings from a 2005 Global Insight Study showing that consumers saved $2,329 per household per year from 1985 to 2004. The company's ability to ring out efficiencies to lower prices has been imitated by the Megas that followed on its heals during the 1980s and 1990s. Today, price optimization software and forecasting analysis assist the Megas in the perfection of their pricing decisions.

Inventory Management

Technological advances have allowed the Megas to become masters of inventory management. Sam Walton anticipated the need to implement an inventory management system in the mid-1960s to address what he called an "absentee ownership" situation. The essential question concerned Wal-Mart's ability to manage its inventory as the number of stores grew and central management was no longer able to monitor what was happening in each store. The key is information. Computer technology appeared on the scene at just the right time for Wal-Mart and for the other Megas. Former Wal-Mart executive Abe Marks stated, "without the computer, Sam Walton could not have done what he's done. He could not have built a retailing empire the size of what he's built, the way he built it."[11] This applies to all of the other Megas as well. The key weapon in their arsenal of control is timely and accurate information about inventory, including what items are selling, what items are sitting on the shelf, and what needs to be ordered, marked down, or replaced.

As information technology has advanced, inventory management systems have become increasingly sophisticated. Today, the Megas utilize Electronic Data Interchange (EDI), which manufacturers can use to control the content and flow of material in their supply chain, to track sales, and then to replenish stock as needed. EDI involves direct communication between the computer systems of both the Megas and their vendors. Before access to the Internet was widespread, this communication took place through privately owned networks, but now it often occurs online through Web applications.

Another technology that is further empowering the Megas is radio-frequency identification (RFID). This technology consists of little microchips, called tags, placed in the packaging of products that then can be traced from the factory floor right into the customer's house. RFID allows retailers to know exactly how much of a product is sitting on its shelf so that they can order more from their vendors precisely when it is needed. Wal-Mart required its top 100 suppliers to use tags and Sam's Club required all its vendors to tag each full single-item pallet or pay a $2 to $3 dollar fee for Sam's Club to tag the pallet. Despite setbacks, the company is still pursuing this technology.

Implementation of RFID is expensive. A study by Forrester Research, Inc. estimated that a typical supplier would have to shell out $9 million dollars to make it work. The costs involved make more sense for high-margin items. Paul Freeman, the RFID program director for Best Buy, explained, "We have found with our suppliers that the tag cost is not nearly the deal breaker that it is for consumer product goods manufacturing. And a lot of our cases have a single item, so we can get some traction at the item-level."[12]

Outsourcing

The ability to have products manufactured overseas at a fraction of what it would cost in the United States has been a huge boon to the Megas. Dramatic savings through cheap overseas labor pushes prices down and keeps them low. This process fits in nicely with the way Megas make their money—that is, through rapid stock-turn brought about by low prices and effective merchandising. Globalization has freed the Megas from constraints imposed by domestic manufacturers. If a company cannot produce a product according to specifications and at the right prices, then someone else can or the Mega can have it made to order in an overseas factory.

Commoditization

In the present environment, firms that create innovative products or services that are substantially different from those of competitors run the risk of selling something of superior value that is perceived to be only ordinary by the marketplace. The Megas are experts at making this happen. An innovative product sitting on the shelf next to average products with similar promotional claims runs the risk of premature commoditization.

Commoditization is the transformation of a non-commodity product into a commodity. A commodity is a product where consumers perceive no difference between the offerings of different suppliers or manufacturers, other than price. . . . A commoditized product is

characterized by low-margins, high competition and low importance of brands.[13]

In December 1995, when Toshiba announced that it had
worked out the final design of the DVD format with Sony, it
stated that the cost of players would eventually drop to between
$500 and $700.[14] Within seven years, the DVD player was a
commodity. Former Circuit City Chief Executive Officer Alan
McCollough said at a 2003 shareholders' meeting, "Who would
have thought that five years ago when DVD was introduced at
$600 [a player], that today the market share leader would be
Wal-Mart? Because a DVD player is now $39 and you can throw
it in a cart."[15]

Private-Label Goods

The commoditization of consumer products and the diminishment
of brand value that accompanies it have provided an opening for
the Megas to create and sell their own brands at lower prices
than those of name brands. With no middlemen or vendors to
pay, the Mega ends up with superior profit margins, as much as
20 percent higher than what they earn on a name-brand product.[16] Growth in the purchase of private-label products is increasing, with a 10.2 percent jump from 2007 to 2008.[17] Economic
shocks, recession, energy costs, and the economic challenges
resulting from personal, corporate, and government debt likely
will encourage this trend.

THE WORLD AS IT IS

Present-day Mega-distributors exert control over unsuspecting
producers because of an inherent contradiction. Moving a large
volume of products at a high rate of speed has been the money-
making formula of distributors since the days following the Civil
War. A stock-turn of five with margins of 2 percent equals profits
of 10 percent each year. In contrast, manufacturers' profitability
is based on both the actual value and perceived value of the product by the customer. For the Megas, it is about stock-turn, but for
producers it is (at least potentially) about how customers view the
innovated product or service.

The visible hand of managerial capitalism lives on in the boardrooms of the Mega-distributors. They are the organizers of much of the world's economic activity. Viewing the modern business enterprise as "networks of relationships" implies that firms coordinate activities in a fashion that is mutually beneficial. However, as pointed out in the previous chapter, producing firms often turn over control of their products to Mega-distributors with the faith and hope that sales volume will bring them wealth beyond measure. The Megas are happy to encourage this perspective, even as they exert increasing control over the products and services of the innovating company.

Seeing the world for what it is, rather than what is desired, must be the foundation of any sound business decision. The Megas have mutated during the course of a long history of sales and distribution in the United States. Their business model is sound (for them) and well known. Those who lead companies that produce innovative products and services must know this before deciding what their sales and distribution strategy will be. But most often, for whatever reason, many leaders erroneously believe that the Megas are the best and only option.

NOTES

1. Alfred Chandler, *The Visible Hand: The Managerial Revolution in American Business* (New York: Belknap Press, 1977), p. 223.

2. Ibid., p. 227.

3. Available at http://www.searsarchives.com (accessed March 26, 2009).

4. W. D. Darby, *Story of the Chain Store* (New York: Dry Good Economist, n.d.), p. 9, quoted in John Perkins and Craig Freedman, "Organisational Form and Retailing Development: The Department and the Chain Store, 1860–1940," *Services Industries Journal* (1999): 129.

5. W. S. Hayward and P. White, *Chain Stores: Their Management and Operation*, 3rd ed. (New York: McGraw-Hill), p. 8, quoted in Perkins and Freedman, "Organisational Form and Retailing Development," 130.

6. Nirmalya Kumar, and Jan-Benedict EM Steenkamp, "Retailing: Why Private Labels Succeed," Rediff.com, May 4, 2007.

7. Alfred Chandler, *Scale and Scope* (New York: Belknap Press, 1990), p. 28.

8. Chandler, *The Visible Hand*, p. 336.

9. Sam Walton, *Sam Walton, Made in America: My Story* (New York: Doubleday, 1992), p. 222.

10. Richard Langlois, "Chandler in a Larger Frame: Markets, Transactional Costs, and Organizational Form in History," *Enterprise and Society* 5, no. 3 (2004): 365.

11. Walton, *Sam Walton, Made in America*, p. 111.

12. Mark Robertis, "Best Buy to Deploy RFID," *RFID Journal*, August 31, 2004.

13. R. Wever, C. Boks, H. van Es, and A. Stevels, "Multiple Environmental Benchmarking Data Analysis and Its Implications for Design: A Case Study on Packaging," Ecodesign: Fourth International Symposium on Environmentally Conscious Design and Inverse Manufacturing, 2005, pp. 799–806.

14. Robert Spector, *Category Killers* (Cambridge, MA: Harvard Business School Press, 2005).

15. Laura Heller, "High-Tech Goes Low Price: Mass Contributes to Commoditization—Annual Industry Report Top 150: CE and Entertainment," *DSN Retailing Today*, July 7, 2003.

16. MSNBC, "Slowdown Fuels Sales of Private Labels," MSN News, December 8, 2008.

17. Elaine Wong, "Nielsen: Private Label Deemed Equal to Name Brands," *Brandweek*, November 18, 2008.

Chapter 3

ABANDONING BRAND INTEGRITY

> Never allow a single customer to be more than 10 percent of
> your total business.
> —Donald L. Kaufman

The scope and magnitude of a Mega can quickly consume the brand
equity of individual products and services. Private labels, discounting, lack of service, and mass-market presentation have diluted the
value of American brands. The Distribution Trap has squeezed margins by making products that were, at one time, viewed with respect
easily replaced with either store brands or inexpensive substitutes.
Deep discounting by the Megas has created customers who are
50 percent more price sensitive than they were in the 1970s and
1980s.[1] In fact, the Megas can be viewed as instruments of brand
dilution. The very act of discounting, which is the business model of
the Megas, undermines the entire idea behind a manufacturer's
brand. As marketing guru Phil Kotler puts it, "Brand death is a
problem."

In this chapter, we take an in-depth look at two brands that
have been damaged by the Distribution Trap. The harm caused to
both Levi Strauss & Co. and Goodyear at the hands of mass-
market retailers provides an object lesson in the dangers of plac-
ing one's hopes in the Megas.

LEVI STRAUSS GIVES IT AWAY

If there is such a thing as an iconic American brand, it is Levi
Strauss & Co. Their jeans, ubiquitous for more than a century,

have been at the very center of American culture. Cowboys and aspiring cowboys strap oversized belt buckles to their Levi's in rural Wyoming; hippies and their cultural progeny put on pre-faded versions; and almost everyone in between wears the jeans in some fashion. This is because Levi's jeans are comfortable.

Levi's jeans are the stuff of legend. The American West was won by frontiersmen wrapped in blue. James Dean wore them in *Rebel without a Cause*; they adorned hippies and flower children, and have recently become the bane of George Will and other "adult" dressers. They even played a role in the Cold War. *Time* magazine reported, in 1962, that bureaucrats in the former Soviet Union opposed their corrupting influence. According to *Time*, "There is even a blue-jean fad, to the anger of militant party stalwarts, who note acidly that the blue denim must have been smuggled in from abroad since it is a product not even manufactured in the Soviet Union."[2] Many European adventures were financed by young Americans smuggling jeans into Russia during the dark days of communism.

Levi Strauss is named after its founder, who created the rugged pants for the miners of the California Gold Rush of the 1850s. Strauss hired a tailor to make pants out of the brown canvas he had carried across the country to San Francisco. After he ran out of material, he was able to source a new supply that originated in the town of Nimes, in France. This material, known as *serge de Nimes*, was anglicized into the simple word "denim." Strauss colored the fabric blue, and then he and his successors scrambled for a century to keep up with sales.

Levi Strauss & Co. had sales of $2.4 million in 1880. Innovations, such as fastening seams with rivets and branding its "waist-high overalls" with numbers—the first number was the now-famous "501"—coupled with an exclusive reliance on more expensive white seamstresses (Chinese labor having been blackballed after the San Francisco riots of 1877), meant that the company had to produce quality products that would command a higher price. During the first half of the 20th century, the firm struggled against both adversarial economic conditions and a lack of visionary leadership. Nonetheless, circumstances helped the company to break out of its regional market. Visits to western dude ranches by easterners during the 1930s, coupled with the appearance of blue jeans in hundreds of Hollywood westerns, created a mystique around this unique product.

During World War II, the U.S. government declared Levi's to be essential to the war effort and made them available exclusively to defense workers. Pent-up consumer demand after the war created an ongoing product shortage. With only five factories, Levi Strauss was forced to implement a distribution program that favored the intermediaries and retailers that it had worked with during the preceding decades. In 1948, company profits were more than $1 million dollars on 4 million pair of jeans.

In the 1950s, Levi Strauss & Co. became a market-driven company. Noticing that America was in the midst of a baby boom, it shifted its attention toward the youth market, emphasizing that its pants were for play, not for work. The firm's sales force became national in scope, focusing on urban rather than rural areas. Numerous innovations followed, including zippers instead of the five-button fly, preshrunk denim jeans, stretch denim, corduroys, and permanent press. Campus rebellion and countercultural conformity were huge windfalls for Levi's. The firm grew at an astonishing pace. From 1963 to 1966, sales doubled to $152 million. In 1968, the firm had sales of $200 million. It was now the sixth-largest clothing producer in the United States. Still, it was unable to keep up with demand.

Despite domestic and international challenges in the 1970s, sales topped $1 billion in 1974 and then doubled in just four years. In the 1980s, Levi Strauss & Co. made its first foray into the mass market. Deals were struck with JCPenney and Sears. In 1982, the company shuttered nine plants and eliminated 2,000 jobs. Despite heavy advertising, alliances with the high-end fashion market, and an Olympic tie-in in 1984, profits were down 50 percent by the middle of the decade. Levi's was able to dig itself out of this hole with new products, including Dockers, and through innovative finishes, such as stonewashing and bleaching. Distribution in the 1990s was extended to upscale stores, like Macy's, as well as company-operated stand-alone Dockers stores and Levi's stores. By 1996, the firm was debt free, had robust operations throughout Europe, was expanding into developing economies such as India and Eastern Europe, and had earnings in excess of $700 million for the decade.[3]

In 2000, Levi Strauss & Co. used a Securities and Exchange Commission (SEC) filing to outline its precarious financial condition. Since its peak in 1996, the firm had closed twenty-nine plants, eliminated 18,500 jobs, and watched profits shrink from $411.5 million in 1997 to just $5.4 million in 1999. The amazing $7.1 billion in sales that had occurred in 1996 had dropped to $5.1 billion. The firm's implosion was attributed to massive debt incurred in 1985, when it went private in a leveraged buyout, high operating costs due to American manufacturing operations, and the derailment of a highly touted employee incentive plan that was introduced during the peak year of 1996. The idea was to reward employees with a one-time bonus that would be equal to one year's pay. The cost was $750 million.[4]

Compounding Levi's difficulties was the altered competitive environment that the firm found itself in at the end of the 20th century. Competition in the 1990s was fierce. Levi's products were positioned above low-end alternatives sold by Sears and JCPenny's, but they were below newer upscale brands produced by Calvin Klein and Tommy Hilfiger Corp. Peter Sealey, a former marketing executive at Coca-Cola and an adjunct professor at the University of California–Berkeley, told the *Los Angeles Times*, "They've allowed the brand image to become something that's not relevant anymore. The worst thing you can do is to get caught in the middle."[5]

A 2003 article in the *Houston Chronicle* said of Levi Strauss, "revenues have been falling for the last six years, and pressure is mounting, analysts say, for the company to produce results or risk becoming a statistic in another American institution—bankruptcy."[6] David Bergen, Levi's senior vice president, stated that the company was caught in the "jaws of death."[7] Levi's was on its way out, or so it seemed.

In 2003, the iconic brand, the inventor of blue jeans, the industry leader, finally cried uncle and began selling through mass-market retailers. The first deal was signed with Wal-Mart. After years of resisting the pull of the Megas, Levi Strauss & Co. acted as if it had no choice but to throw in its lot with the big discounters. Levi Strauss was tempted by the potentially huge sales opportunity that Wal-Mart presented. Kurt Barnard, the publisher of the *Retail Forecasting* newsletter, said:

> The company has been in grave, grave danger for five or six years, and they finally did the one thing—which, I believe, spells survival. That was the deal with Wal-Mart. . . . Where else do you get access to 100 million new customers? The exposure is absolutely unparalleled.[8]

Harry Bernard, an executive at the retail consulting firm Colton Berhnard, summed it up, "They'll get the volume they'll need to survive."[9] Levi's launched its Signature line of jeans at Wal-Mart on

July 22, 2003, and by December, jeans were also placed in Target stores. The Signature line did not have Levi's traditional insignias—the distinctive Red Tab, two-horses leather patch, or stitching on the pocket. The jeans retailed for $23 with a "roll-back" price of around $19.50.[10] Given that the average off-brand price of jeans at Wal-Mart was around $15, the Signature line was a premium product for the discount market segment. Levi Strauss hoped that the scaled-down product, along with the absence of the Red Tab, would adequately differentiate Signature from Levi's core products. Levi president and Chief Executive Officer (CEO) Phil Marineau acknowledged the concern of the company's traditional retail customers when he said that they were "worried about cannibalization of Levi's [core product], particularly from Signature" and, as a result, was "managing Levi's and Dockers orders and inventory very conservatively."[11]

Levi Strauss & Co. completely reengineered its supply chain to fulfill the needs of mass-market customers. The company adopted sophisticated forecasting and product-tracking technologies. Using a "dashboard" that sits on the desks of executives, managers can track a specific product from the factory, to the distribution center, to the individual store. Said one Levi executive, "When I first got here, I didn't see anything. . . . Now I can drill down to the product level."[12] Levi Strauss also expanded its distribution, adding three "pool points" that facilitated product dispersal to Wal-Mart distribution centers and supercenters. In addition, the firm implemented technology to facilitate electronic data interchange as well as other collaborative communications software. A cross-functional team was put together to ensure that these logistics efforts worked properly.

Levi's presence at Wal-Mart gave a big boost to the Mega's efforts to bring name brands into the store. "They do like the name," said consultant Walter Loeb. "They do like to be able to say they carry the Levi brand or they carry the Wrangler brand because it gives credibility to their business."[13] Signature had a sluggish start. Wal-Mart complained that the inventory turn was slower than anticipated. After three months, the disgruntled Mega slashed the price of men's jeans from $23 to $19.[14]

In 2003, Signature represented 8 percent of Levi's sales in the United States and 6 percent worldwide. In 2004, it jumped to 14.5 percent and 9.7 percent, respectively. Wal-Mart executives were pleased with the result. Levi's, now positioned as a mass-market premium brand, represented the "high end" of the retailer's denim offerings. Wal-Mart also sold Wrangler jeans for $15 to $18 and its own private label for $9.99. The Levi's cachet helped to pull people into the stacks of denim produced by the three different companies.[15] By 2006, it was Dockers, not Signature, that was the bright spot for Levi Strauss and Co. This was ironic, given previous attempts to jettison this line.[16]

At the beginning of 2006, Wal-Mart decided to use shelf space in its apparel section for its proprietary brands. Never mind that Levi's had reconfigured its entire supply chain to create a new brand for Wal-Mart. Levi's 2006 SEC filing stated the following:

> Our ability to maintain retail floor space, market share and sales in these channels depends on our ability to offer differentiated and exclusive products and to increase retailer profitability on our products, which could have an adverse impact on our margins. In addition, recent efforts by mass channel retailers in the United States to expand their private label offerings may reduce floor space devoted to our Levi Strauss Signature® products, which could have an adverse impact on our sales. For example, we experienced such impacts in 2006 as a result of actions taken by Wal-Mart to increase its private label women's business.[17]

Signature was not doing well. The company stopped selling the product in Europe because of the insufficiency of mass-market channels. The 2007 Annual Financial Report stated,

> The Signature by Levi Strauss & Co. brand had a difficult year, as expected. The brand is being overhauled to align with our mass retail customer's evolving apparel merchandising strategies. The plans we have developed with them will give the brand a fresh look and a new presence at retail for fall 2008.[18]

Third-quarter results for 2008 were revealing: "Higher net revenues reflected growth in each of the company's three regions. The increase in net revenues was primarily driven by currency, the addition of brand-dedicated retail stores worldwide, and sales growth at existing stores."[19] And in their corporate filing for 2009, Levi Strauss stated that it might not be able to increase sales through the mass market because of private-label competition and because, in the mass-market channel, there was a reduction in "fixture spaces and purchases of brands that do not meet their [the Megas] mass market requirements."[20]

Ironically, it had been the mass market that was supposed to save the company. An article in the *Irish Times* summarized the strategic miscalculation that tipped Levi's off its perch:

> Up until the mid-1990s, Levi's jeans were seen as an essential fashion item. But then the industry underwent a seismic shift, as denim came to be seen as a luxury item, with brands such as 7 for All Mankind and True Religion selling their jeans for up to six times what a pair of Levi's cost and distributing them through luxury boutiques and department stores.
>
> Instead of jumping on the bandwagon, Levi's failed to respond to changing consumer tastes and suffered. It clung firmly to its position as a mid-priced manufacturer, despite the fact that the denim business was becoming polarized between the luxury and the discount end. In fact, Levi's did not introduce its own premium denim line, Capital E, until 2006, long after the luxury trend had first emerged.[21]

The Megas have demonstrated a phenomenal ability to dominate businesses and transform entire industries. Unfortunately, this domination and transformation has left many of American's producers in weakened, and even subservient, positions relative to large-scale distributors. Like Levi Strauss, the story of Goodyear illustrates the diminishing aura of once-dominant brands and the power that the Megas now have over the manufacturing sector.

GOODYEAR: THE RUBBER HITS THE PARKING LOT

Perhaps no other company is as emblematic of American industrial might as is The Goodyear Tire and Rubber Company. With its ubiquitous dealerships, highly visible blimps, and widely respected product, Goodyear dominated the tire market for most of the 20th century. It is difficult to fathom that this icon of American manufacturing has been nearly undone in recent years by its negligent embrace of the Megas—a negligence involving the rejection of decades of carefully nurturing, maintaining, and expanding one of the most successful dealer networks in American business history.

The Goodyear Tire & Rubber Company, the pioneer tire company and the industry leader for nearly 100 years, was pushed into the Distribution Trap in the mid-1990s. For years, the firm

cautiously managed an extensive and effective sales network, consisting of more than 5,000 authorized dealers. Then, in the mid-
1990s, as part of a reorganization effort, it abandoned its dealers
and began to sell through Sears, Wal-Mart, and Montgomery
Ward. Predictably, the dealers did not take this sitting down but
linked their fortunes to other brands, like Michelin, Pirelli, and
Bridgestone. As a result, Goodyear lost a global network of faithful, committed dealers, and ended up selling a product perceived
by consumers as just another tire sold at discount stores. Bob
Davis, a former Goodyear dealer in New Hampshire, stated,
"You'd buy a tire from them one month, and the next month the
price would be 20 percent lower or higher. . . . It was just too
hard to do business with Goodyear."[22]

The Goodyear Tire & Rubber Company was founded in 1898,
when Frank A. Seiberling borrowed $3,500 to buy a former
strawboard factory in Akron, Ohio. Named after Charles Goodyear, the inventor of the rubber vulcanization process, the firm
grew to 30,000 employees and had a pre-Depression production
high of 837,000 tires in April 1920. By 1928, despite Depression
era challenges, the company had sales of $250 million and opera-
tions in 145 countries.[23]

Goodyear's contemporary use of mass distributors was pres-
aged during the early years when it entered into a distribution
agreement with Sears, Roebuck and Company. The deal was
simple—Goodyear charged Sears for the cost of producing tires
plus a profit margin of 6 percent. In what was to become a
famous antitrust case, the tire maker was accused, in 1936, of
being in violation of the Clayton Act, an antitrust law enacted in
1914. Unlike the Sherman Antitrust Act, which was concerned
with attempts to monopolize commerce, the Clayton Act focused
on practices deemed to interfere with fair competition. Section 2
of the Act stated, "it shall be unlawful for any person engaged in
[interstate] commerce to discriminate in price between different
purchasers . . . where the effect of such discrimination may be to
substantially lessen competition or tend to create a monopoly in
any line of [interstate] commerce."[24] A review article analyzing
the law in 1932 stated:

> It is difficult to escape the conclusion, at this point, that Section 2 is
> a nuisance that may be used by a disgruntled customer to present to
> a judicial tribunal the substantial conflicts of interest and questions
> of merchandising policy considered above, to be resolved by the

court as best it can by the interpretation of the technical and ill-conceived language of the section. It must also be apparent that the trade associations and the Federal Trade Commission, in so far as they are attempting to stamp out price cutting by means of Section 2, have chosen an instrument that is unwieldy and ill-designed for their purpose.[25]

In 1936, the Federal Trade Commission issued an order forcing the tire company to end its arrangement with Sears. Goodyear appealed. After the Act was amended later that year, and became even more draconian, Goodyear executives decided to terminate their relationship with the retailer. The company's use of mass-market distributors would not be revived until the 1980s, when it once again began selling its tires through Sears. Ironically, the appeal that the tire company filed came out in its favor in 1939.

The failure of the Sears deal meant that Goodyear had to develop its own marketing channels. As a result, the tire maker spent decades in control of its distribution. At its peak in the 1980s, the firm operated more than 1,000 company-owned stores, which produced 27 percent of sales. Six hundred franchised dealers generated 8 percent of sales, and 4,400 independent dealers produced 50 percent of sales. Franchise dealers were simply new Goodyear dealers that graduated to independent status after completing three years of training by the company in the areas of business, finance, and operations.

Goodyear built its multi-million-dollar enterprise by creating the most effective dealership network in the United States. For most of its history, its dealers sold only Goodyear tires. The unwritten agreement went something like this: You sell only Goodyear tires, and we'll take care of you. As long as your performance is satisfactory, we will provide you with an exclusive sales territory. If you are the Goodyear dealer in North Platte, Nebraska, we will sell tires only through you. If your performance is off, we will talk to you about how to fix things before we open either a company-owned store or a separate dealership. In exchange, Goodyear dealers sold only Goodyear tires. At least, this was how it was supposed to work. In 1989, 70 percent of the dealers sold only Goodyear tires. By 1991, the number had dropped to 50 percent. The other brands carried by dealers were typically used as lower-priced alternatives.[26]

The Goodyear tire network was so loyal to the company that when the British financier James Goldsmith attempted a hostile takeover in 1986, the dealers were his most vocal opponents. The company was able to beat off the takeover attempt through the combined efforts of the alarmed dealers, the citizenry of Akron (where Goodyear is headquartered), and several Goodyear blimps literally buzzing the city like bombers on the lookout for invaders.

The high debt load resulting from the battle with Goldsmith was the ostensible reason behind Goodyear's decision to begin selling to Sears in 1992. This decision was followed by deals with Wal-Mart and Sam's Club.[27] In June 1991, Stan Gault, the former CEO of Rubbermaid and a Goodyear board member, took over the battered tire giant. Gault had experienced fabulous career success. Touted as a "miracle man" on Wall Street, he was popular in the investment community because of his career history. During his eleven years at Rubbermaid, the company had quadrupled in size with earnings growing sixfold. "He's a real tough cookie when it comes to costs," a former associated reported.[28]

Sears had been attempting to get Goodyear to supply them with tires since 1989. Concern about the dealer network forestalled action until the Gault ascendancy. With his marketing background and previous experience selling through the Mega-distributors, Gault provided about 20 percent of Sear's tire inventory. The next deal was inked with Wal-Mart, which began selling a line called Viva in 1994.[29] Discount Tire and Montgomery Ward followed, with the latter selling two exclusive tire lines. Gault stated at the time that the arrangement with Montgomery Ward was an attempt to "expand distribution to new customers."[30]

Stan Gault undermined the Goodyear dealer network. In 1992, half of the 4,400 independent Goodyear dealers sold only Goodyear tires. The other half generally sold only one additional brand. Gault implemented a number of cost-cutting measures and strategic initiatives, but his decision to begin selling tires on the mass market was the one with the most far-reaching consequences. The abandonment of the dealers did not come about as the result of analysis, executive discussions, or boardroom debate. Rather, Gault simply made the decision. "Stan was an outsider," stated a former Goodyear executive, who spoke to us on condition of anonymity, "he never really appreciated the culture that had been created around the dealer network." The decision to begin selling to the mass market was, the executive claimed, "Stan's decision. He didn't consult with the rest of us, and no one challenged his decision. When Stan's mind was made up, he wouldn't budge. And no one was about to publicly disagree with him." To emphasize the newly adopted mass-market approach in which all channels would be used, Gault personally sold a set of tires to a pilot while flying to Chicago to join Sears executives for a press conference announcing the agreement.[31]

In the immediate aftermath of the decision to supply Sears, Goodyear's market share increased from 15 percent to 16 percent, largely reflecting Sear's inventory buildup. Initially, dealers responded to Goodyear's embrace of the mass-market discounters with despair. One dealer said, "We went with them through thick and thin, and now they're going to drown us."[32] Not only did the dealers have to contend with new competitors, but the high-velocity, lower-price approach of the Megas meant that they had to lower their prices, resulting in lower margins for everyone.[33]

The dealers did not sit idly by as the rug was pulled out from under them. According to Manny Dracakis, a former Goodyear dealer and the owner of All-American Tire and Service in Cincinnati, "After someone punches you in the face a few times, you say, 'Enough is enough.'"[34] With the delicate relationship between Goodyear and its dealer network violated, the dealers soon found other paramours. Instead of selling Goodyear tires exclusively, they began to carry multiple brands. Pam Fitzgerald, the vice president of a large dealership in Florida, was quoted in the *Wall Street Journal* as saying, "We sell what we think will give the customer the best value, and that's not necessarily Goodyear."[35] The adoption of new brands by this dealership reduced the sales of Goodyear tires by 20 percent.

For its part, Sears used Goodyear tires as an inducement to attract customers, but it then pushed its own store brand, Roadhandler, as well as other private labels. In 2000, Nashville-based Bridgestone Americas Tire Operations recalled millions of original equipment and replacements tires that had been identified as potentially unsafe by the National Highway Transportation Safety Board. It appeared as if the very survival of the company was at stake. Yet, two years later, the firm reported a $135 million operating profit due to increased sales of both Bridgestone and Firestone tires. During the same period, Goodyear suffered a 12.1 percent decline in North American sales and a dramatic drop in operating earnings—from $80 million down to $10 million. According to an editorial in the industry journal, *Tire Business*, the divergence in fortunes was attributable to the difference in how the companies had managed their dealer networks. Bridgestone, and its predecessor Firestone, had worked hard to create a loyal dealer network so that, when the bad times came, the dealers would stick with the company. In contrast, Goodyear dealers had been stiffed by the manufacturer since the days of Stan Gault. The editorial stated:

> Many Goodyear dealers are angry with the company and don't feel the loyalty they once did to the tire maker. But there is no reason why Goodyear, which once enjoyed a dealer following second to none, can't regain that loyalty. It must again make independent dealers its number one priority. Ever since the Akron-based tire maker began, years ago, to expand distribution beyond its own company stores and independent dealers, it has been losing momentum. Goodyear's independent tire dealers are one of the tire company's greatest assets. They stand on the front lines and more often than not determine what the retail tire customer buys. They can help re-energize the company. The sooner Goodyear recognizes this, the better.[36]

Despite the entreaties of industry observers, Goodyear continued to push its product though the Megas. By 2003, it had lost control of distribution and was selling what was widely perceived to be a commodity product on the mass market. In the tire business, loyalty was a fixture of a bygone era, like rotary phones or eight-track tape players. By this time, Gault had retired, and a new CEO was promising to make up with the dealers. The problem was not so much about bad relationships but about how Goodyear allowed itself to lose control over the distribution of its product.

But what of the other big tire manufacturers? Did they fall prey to the Distribution Trap? Bridgestone still has a loyal dealer network. It sells 85 percent of its tires through independent dealers and company-owned stores. While Bridgestone *does* sell through Sears Auto Centers and Sam's Club, it eschews Wal-Mart and most other mass-market outlets.[37] Michelin works closely with dealers and also sells on the mass market, but because its tires are positioned as premium products in the marketplace, the Megas are less able to squeeze them on margins. Research undertaken by Michelin indicates that customers who buy either Michelin or BFGoodrich brands spend an average of $388 when they purchase tires. That is 30 percent more than the average spent on other brands.[38]

Gault retired from Goodyear at the end of 1995. Net income for the year stood at $611 million. It was a great year, adding to Gault's reputation as a turnaround expert. By 2001, the company was in the red and has stayed there for most of the decade. During this time, it has had one of the worst-performing stocks on the Standard & Poor's (S&P) 500 Index. While many factors have undoubtedly contributed to the breakdown of the company, the commoditization of Goodyear tires, due to the jettisoning of a loyal distribution network, has surely played a large role. Goodyear lost control of its distribution and has yet to recover.[39]

An interesting fact: Stan Gault began serving as a member of Wal-Mart's board in 1997.

NOTES

1. Leonard M. Lodish and Carl F. Mela, "If Brands Are Built Over Years, Why Are They Managed Over Quarters?" *Harvard Business Review*, July-August 2007.

2. "The Liberal Life," *Time*, February 16, 1962, available at http://www.time.com/time/magazine/article/0,9171,829038,00.html.

3. "Levi Strauss & Co., Funding Universe," available at http://www.fundinguniverse.com/company-histories/Levi-Strauss-amp-Co-Company-History.html.

4. Andrea Orr, "Levi Must Work Out of Tight Fit: Wal-Mart Deal May End Slide in Revenues," *Houston Chronicle*, September 18, 2003, p. 4.

5. Greg Johnson, "Troubles at Levi Strauss Revealed in SEC Filing," *Los Angeles Times*, May 5, 2000, p. C-1.

6. Orr, "Levi Must Work Out of Tight Fit."

7. Kim Girard, "Supply Chain Partnerships: How Levi's Got Its Jeans into Wal-Mart," *CIO*, July 15, 2003, available at http://www.cio.com/articles/print/31948.

8. Orr, "Levi Must Work Out of Tight Fit."

9. Girard, "Supply Chain Partnerships."

10. Katherine Bowersne, "Levi's Hits Mass," *Women's Wear Daily*, December 9, 2003, p. 17.

11. Ibid.

12. Ibid.

13. E. Clark, "Changing Retail Market: Vendors Eye Discounters to Bolster Bottom Line," *Women's Wear Daily*, March 16, 2005, pp. 1–10.

14. "Fitting In: In Bow to Retailers' New Clout, Levi Strauss Makes Alterations," June 17, 2004, p. A-1.

15. Sally Beatty, "At Levi Strauss Trouble Comes from All Angles," *Wall Street Journal*, October 10, 2003.

16. Ray A. Smith, "At Levi Strauss, Dockers Are In: Rise in Sales Is Bright Spot, as Company Tries to Mend Its Jeans," *Wall Street Journal*, February 14, 2007.

17. SEC Filing, Form 10-K, 2006, p. 14, available at http://www.sec.gov/Archives/edgar/data/94845/000095013406002782/f17124e10vk.htm.

18. Levi Strauss & Co., 2007 Annual Report, available at http://www.levistrauss.com/Downloads/AR_2007.pdf.

19. Levi Strauss & Co., "Levi Strauss & Co. Announces Third-Quarter 2008 Financial Results" (press release), 2008.

20. SEC Filing, Form 10-K, 2009, p. 12, available at http://www.sec.gov/Archives/edgar/data/94845/000089161809000035/f51209e10vk.htm.

21. Michael Appel, "Levi Strauss Signature: The Birth or Demise of a Brand?" *Retail Merchandiser* 44, no. 5 (May 2004): 58; "Competition in Denim Market Makes Levi's a Fashion Victim." *Irish Times*. August 4, 2008, p. 19.

22. Kevin Kelleher, "Giving Dealers a Raw Deal," CNNMoney.com, December 1, 2004, available at http://money.cnn.com/magazines/business2/business2_archive/2004/12/01/8192549/index.htm.

23. Available at http://www.goodyear.com/corporate/history/history_byyear.html.

24. Breck P. McAllister, "Sales Policies and Price Discrimination under the Clayton Act," *Yale Law Journal* 41, no. 4 (1932): 519.

25. Ibid., pp. 527–528.

26. Bruce Isaacson and John Quelch, "Goodyear: The Aquatred Launch," *Harvard Business School*, case no. 9–594–106, September 7, 1994.

27. Kelleher, "Giving Dealers a Raw Deal."

28. Zachary Schiller, "Goodyear's Miracle Man?" *Business Week*, June 17, 1991, available at http://www.businessweek.com/archives/1991/b321823.arc.htm.

29. "Goodyear Sets Tire Deal," *Wall Street Journal*, November 2, 1993.

30. "Goodyear to Sell Tires at 350 Montgomery Ward & Co. Outlets," *Wall Street Journal*, June 14, 1995.

31. Lloyd Stoyer, "A Juggling Act: Dealer/Supplier Relationships Take Work as Other Parties Look Out for Their Own Best Interests," *Modern Tire Dealer*, April 2008.

32. Dana Milibank, "Independent Goodyear Dealers Rebel: Decision to Sell through Sears Proves Unpopular," *Wall Street Journal*, July 8, 1992.

33. Stoyer. "A Juggling Act."

34. Kelleher, "Giving Dealers a Raw Deal."

35. Milibank, "Independent Goodyear Dealers Rebel."

36. Editorial, *Tire Business*, November 11, 2002.

37. Stoyer, "A Juggling Act."

38. Bruce Davis, "Michelin Unit Attempts to Satisfy Dealer Complaints," *Rubber and Plastics News* 36, no. 12 (2007).

39. Goodyear Tire & Rubber Co., Financial Statement, available at http://moneycentral.msn.com/investor (accessed September 18, 2008); Ann and Elizabeth Harrow, "Worst 10-Year Performers: The Goodyear Tire & Rubber Company Skids Out," July 26, 2008, available at http://moneycentral.msn.com/investor/invsub/results/statemnt.aspx?Symbol=gt &lstStatement=10YearSummary&stmtView; www.bloggingstocks.com, available at http://www.bloggingstocks.com/2008/07/26/worst-10-year-performers-the-goodyear-tire-and-rubber-company-ski.

Chapter 4

TURNING YOUR INNOVATIONS
INTO COMMODITIES

Control your destiny or somebody else will.

—anonymous

Innovation has been all the rage in popular and academic circles for a long time. Recently, educators have been developing and implementing curricula that emphasize science and math for the purpose of keeping America at the top of the innovation ladder. At universities, new masters of business administration (MBA) programs and executive education courses focused on integrating innovation within the corporate culture are incredibly popular. Companies of all sizes have introduced innovation departments or divisions. The position of chief innovation officer (CIO) has become an increasingly fashionable job title. A recent search on monster.com revealed 13,000 management positions with the word "innovation" in the title. Technology transfer is sold as the link between academe and the private sector. Best-selling books by management gurus are in lockstep agreement that innovation is *the* hope for most companies as firms seek to avoid commoditization and stay ahead of the competition.

The conventional wisdom holds that innovation is essential for many companies that seek sustainable competitive advantage. The argument is that globalization, homogenous markets, hyper-competition, and lower costs can rapidly turn many innovative products and services into commodities, thereby disallowing companies time to recoup the cost of bringing the innovation to market. In response, innovation is pushed from all corners as the best way for companies to stay ahead of the competition and deliver high value to customers. However, the practice of innovation often comes up short.

The problem is not a lack of innovative ideas (77,501 patents were granted in the United States in 2008), nor is it spending on research and development (R&D). In the current economic downturn, despite the plunge in revenues for many firms, spending on R&D has remained fairly consistent.[1] For many business leaders, innovation is viewed as the best way to ensure growth once market conditions begin to improve. Examples of companies creating great innovations during turbulent economic times include DuPont's invention of shatterproof plastic and creation of nylons, and Kraft Food's introduction of macaroni-and-cheese dinners and formulation of Miracle Whip. These products were developed during the Great Depression. During the recession of 2001, Apple Computer, Inc., introduced the iPod.[2]

Why do so many innovations fail? While there are many possibilities, one explanation is that developing an innovation is simply the first step in a two-step process, and if the second step is missed, all the blood, sweat, tears, and money that were poured into the product in the first place are likely to be wasted. Dishearteningly, many firms simply do not demonstrate much interest in capturing the real value of their innovations, especially as they move into the second step—the sale and distribution of their products and processes. Instead of reaping rewards for their efforts, companies have allowed the Mega-distributors to take over the second step, thereby accelerating the process of commoditization.

With the dream of huge sales and a bigger market, innovative firms lose control as their innovations move out of the laboratory or factory and into the marketplace. The misstep of neglecting sales and distribution accelerates the path of commoditization for the innovation. Many companies that, at one time, built innovative products that could command high prices have abandoned this strategy, instead adopting the "volume at all costs" approach. This has occurred through a systematic process by which the Megas use their disproportionate size and buying power to disable the strategic imperatives of the innovative companies that do business with them.

As discussed in Chapter 1, the origins of the current arrangement began several decades ago, when manufacturers seemed to lose interest in managing sales and distribution in favor of a new managerial paradigm that emphasized core competencies (innovation, technology, operational effectiveness, and outsourcing). By identifying and exploring their internal capabilities, businesses believed they would be able to focus more effectively on creating better innovations for new markets—resulting in significant benefits for customers. It was assumed that new innovations produced at a lower cost would be the ultimate result for companies that pursued this strategy. By catering to the mass market, however, innovative companies allowed Mega-distributors to capture the value of their products and services, even as the Megas imposed costs and changes in strategic direction and operational control. Too often, the innovations of producers pass from their ownership and control into a form of property held, for all practical purposes, in the hands of the Mega.

Innovations sold by the Megas create a great deal of exposure for the brand being sold, resulting in many customers for the Megas and allowing the Megas to profit handsomely. As products become successful and new facilities (and debt) are created to keep up with consumer demand, the Megas insist on greater price reductions and, in the end, companies end up working like dogs to keep up with the demands of their "partners"—all the while watching their innovations being treated more and more like commodities.

THE EXAMPLE FROM DETROIT

For decades, Detroit's Big Three dominated hundreds of small and geographically isolated car dealerships. Dealers functioned in restricted areas and were not allowed to sell competing brands. Beginning in the late 1970s, to boost lagging sales, the Big Three grew their number of dealers and permitted existing ones to sell other brands of automobiles if those brands did not constitute direct competition with Ford Motor Company, General Motors Corporation (GMC), or Chrysler Group LLC. For example, Ford dealers could sell GMC trucks and Chrysler dealers could sell Pontiacs. Over time, the ability of manufacturers to exert control over their now multibrand dealers began to erode because everyone was selling everything. The manufacturers, companies that prided themselves on new designs with each model year rollout, did not intervene because they were afraid of losing short-term sales and alienating long-term customers. The shift of power away from the manufacturer/innovator to the dealers was now under way. The inevitable outcome was that, instead of an exclusive, dedicated dealer who sold only one line of vehicles, dealerships were now able to evolve into superstores, selling multiple brands. The biggest auto dealer in the country, today, is AutoNation, which sells almost every brand that is available in the United States.

When Detroit opened up the Pandora's box of multibrand dealerships, it was left with only two potential options that would allow it to regain control over distribution. First, it could drop unruly dealers and create a completely new sales and distribution network. While straightforward from a business point of view, the Big Three were unable to do this because of state laws and regulations designed to maintain manufacturer-dealer agreements. V. Kasturi Rangan summarizes the situation this way:

> By the end of the 1980s, dealers had gained a huge degree of independence from U.S. manufacturers. Dealers could add imported car brands that were, in some cases, stronger than their corresponding U.S. nameplates, and dealers had made headway in creating state laws to protect them from heavy-handed franchising practices, including the termination of dealers. The automakers had significant clout at the federal level, but at the state level, the dealers held significant sway. Automobile dealers accounted for only 1 to 2 percent of all retail outlets, but, on average, they contributed 20 percent of states' retail revenues and consequently 3 percent of all state tax revenues.[3]

In small-town America, car dealerships are often the largest businesses in a given legislative district. State representatives were not interested in allowing Detroit to dismantle these local sources of employment and tax revenue.

The second option was to create more dealerships, often near the territories of existing dealers. This ultimately led to lower profitability for dealerships as they competed with each other for the same market share as well as increased costs for Detroit because of the need to supply and support underperforming outlets. As multibrand dealerships proliferated, the Big Three thought that the solution to their distribution problems might be in the emergence of e-commerce as a viable channel. However, the political clout of the dealers was not about to be bypassed. By May 2000, thirty-three states had laws prohibiting or restricting manufacturers selling cars online.[4]

The third option for manufacturers was to learn to get along with the new power structure and see their innovative products become commoditized year after year. Detroit had to retain its existing dealer network, and, logically, the evolution of multi-brand dealers continued because firms like AutoNation were able to sell an array of models from different manufactures. For Auto-Nation, a Mega-distributor that represents multiple manufacturers in many states, the only brand that matters is the one serving its purposes at a particular moment. Because dealers like AutoNation manage a portfolio of brands, they are able to quickly adapt and respond to changes in the marketplace. If there is a new model change at Ford that the buying public does not like, or if Ford's innovations are good but are not as good as their competitors, AutoNation can seamlessly shift to selling more popular Chevrolets, Dodges, Hyundais, or Kias. Their customers will still buy, revenues will still come into the Mega-distributor, and the dealership will continue to grow.

Ganley Auto Group is the largest auto dealer in Ohio and one of the top ten in the entire United States. The brands the company sells include BMW, Honda, Hyundai, Isuzu, Mercedes-Benz, Nissan, Subaru, Scion, Suzuki, Toyota, Volkswagen, Chevrolet, Chrysler, Dodge, Ford, Jeep, Lincoln, and Mercury.[5] Is Ganley married to any one brand? No way. The only brand that matters to Ganley is the one that is serving its needs at any particular moment. Ganley can seamlessly shift to selling "better" brands and models at any point.

Ford has spent billions of dollars catching up with the technological lead of Toyota and Nissan. But what happens when the buying public is not excited about Ford products? What can it do? Ford only produces and sells Ford brand automobiles and trucks. The company has borne most, if not all, of the risk—it has dealt with the lawyers and government safety inspectors, spent tens of millions of dollars on engineering tests and designs, conducted thousands of hours of market research, sourced new parts from suppliers, and retooled its manufacturing processes—to bring innovative new products to market. All of this was done in the name of innovation, but because Ford can barely influence its biggest customers like AutoNation in any meaningful way, it is always under pressure to cut costs, pressure suppliers, and, when necessary, distribute jobs offshore. U.S. automakers average a net of 5 percent on sales with profitability ranging from −2.5 to 10 percent.[6]

Only after government bailouts and bankruptcy proceedings were automakers able to gain some control over the sale of their products. In the spring of 2009, with assurances from bankruptcy courts and government bodies, each company cut out nearly 1,000 dealers from its network.

RUBBERMAID ABROGATES CONTROL

Another example of a company falling into the Distribution Trap is Rubbermaid. For years, this firm was admired because it produced a wide range of high-quality storage and related products. The company was directly plugged into customer needs like few other consumer product companies. Ellen Spong, a stay-at-home mom from Canton, Ohio, said, "I remember when Rubbermaid called and asked to spend some time in my house. Two researchers spent the afternoon in the kids' bedroom, looking at how things were packed into the closets and asking questions about possible solutions to all of the kids' stuff." Such attention to understanding how people might use Rubbermaid's products created an industry with a name brand that was admired and respected throughout America. However, by 2008, the company, which had been acquired by Newell ten years before, was firmly ensconced in the commodity business.

Rubbermaid got its start in 1933, when James R. Caldwell and his wife invented twenty-nine products based on deficiencies they experienced in their own kitchen. Caldwell "rang ten doorbells and sold nine dustpans." Buoyed by his success, he was soon making use of department stores to market soap dishes, sink plugs, and drain board mats throughout New England. The new firm merged with Wooster Rubber Company, a struggling Ohio enterprise that had formed in 1920. Wooster Rubber Company, with only $80,000 in sales in 1935, was rejuvenated by the merger, and in 1941, the newly constituted Rubbermaid company had sales of $450,000. By this time, Caldwell had succeeded in marketing twenty-seven of the twenty-nine products he and his wife had envisioned.

Like many businesses during World War II, Rubbermaid switched from producing consumer products to contributing items needed for the war effort. After the war, the company introduced automotive accessories, such as rubber floor mats and cup holders, as well as its previous line of products. But it was not until 1955 that the business began to make products out of plastic, with the introduction of a plastic dishpan in 1956. Soon Rubbermaid marketed industrial and commercial items to restaurants, hotels, and other businesses.

Caldwell retired in the late 1950s. The next major leader of Rubbermaid was Donald E. Noble, a man of amazing vision and managerial abilities. Noble arranged for company stock to be sold on the New York Stock Exchange, pushed for a goal of doubling earnings on a six-year basis (which he was able to pull off), and based the firm's future on its ability to innovate. Product development was the key to this new effort. By 1968, the goal was to have 30 percent of annual sales originate from products introduced within the five previous years.

Like many companies in the 1970s, Rubbermaid began to get into unrelated businesses. It unsuccessfully marketed recreational goods such as snow sleds and motorboats. "We bombed," the vice president of marketing said to a *Wall Street Journal* reporter at the time. Other troubles followed, including problems with the Federal Trade Commission in the 1970s.

Donald Noble retired in 1980. He was replaced by none other than Stan Gault, the man who would later go on to lead Goodyear into the Distribution Trap during the 1990s. Gault cut his teeth at General Electric (GE), where he had been in charge of the appliance division. A Wooster native, he made his way through college by working at Rubbermaid during the summers. Gault set out to quadruple sales by 1990, and he acted quickly. Operations were streamlined. Factories in the Netherlands were closed, the party-plan business (similar to Tupperware) was abandoned, and the automotive division was sold. Eleven percent of management was fired, and half of the company's middle management positions were eliminated. Gault brought in people from GE to fill the top spots in the firm.

A period of aggressive acquisition followed, which included the purchase of MicroComputer Accessories, a computer accessory company, and the Gott Corporation, a producer of insulated coolers and beverage holders. Rubbermaid also entered into joint ventures with Allibert, a producer of outdoor furniture, and DSM N.V., a Dutch chemical manufacturer. In 1989, sales stood at $1.45 billion, four times what they were in 1981 ($350 million).[7] Gault had exceeded his initial goal of quadrupling sales. How did he do this? Two major factors contributed to Rubbermaid's astonishing growth—acquisitions and innovations. The most noteworthy of these was the acquisition of Little Tikes.

Little Tikes

Little Tikes was an innovative company par excellence. In 1970, Thomas G. Murdough was unhappy with what he perceived to be the cheap and poorly made toys that flooded the market during the decade. In response, he founded the Little Tikes Company, based on a technology called rotational molding, which was used to produce large agricultural and chemical containers. Murdough found that molded plastic toys made while using this methodology were more durable than the products then on the market.

The firm used its technology to invent outdoor play equipment in many styles using a large variety of shapes. The rotational molding process facilitated the creation of large surface areas that were durable and with comparatively few parts. As impressive as Murdough's product and process innovations were, his understanding of sales and distribution was even more remarkable.

Murdough believed that he could avoid the deep discounting and low product quality of other toy manufacturers by keeping tight control over distribution. During the 1960s, the strategy of large retailers, like Kmart, was to draw parents into their stores by marketing the most popular toys as loss leaders. As a result, smaller stores were forced to lower their own prices and suffer from low profit margins. These small stores then put pressure on wholesalers, who pushed manufacturers to lower their own prices. The manufacturers managed to do this by compromising on quality. Younger baby boomers can attest to the steady decline in toy quality that occurred during the late 1960s through the 1970s. Compare what this generation says about toys with those who went to grade school in the 1950s.

Murdough was not drawn into the downward quality spiral because he simply refused to do business with large discounters. Instead, he focused on manufacturing innovative products, creating word-of-mouth "buzz" among parents, and building an effective network of independent distributors. The strategy of innovation, in concert with control over sales and distribution, was a phenomenal success.

Murdough sold his company to Rubbermaid for $50 million in 1984, stayed on as president for five years, and then resigned in frustration. He quit because Rubbermaid officials placed unrelenting pressure on him to distribute Little Tikes products through Kmart and Ames. Murdough objected, arguing that heavy promotion in the mass market could lead to short product life cycles. "You saturate the marketplace. . . . That's a big part of the reason the toy industry is flat on its back."[8]

Murdough wanted to "eliminate overkill distribution." A history of Little Tikes describes what happened:

> Mr. Gault resisted, Mr. Murdough says, partly because these same mass merchants devote considerable shelf space to Rubbermaid's vast line of house ware products. "Rubbermaid wants to distribute to every nook and cranny" he [Murdough] says. A decade later, Murdough told *Forbes*, "It turns out we never needed Rubbermaid's money. . . . I was spending all my time just keeping them [Rubbermaid executives] out of my hair."[9]

With Murdough's departure, Gault predicted that Little Tikes would have "its best year ever."[10] Little Tikes began innovating for the mass market. Five additional manufacturing plants were opened, a new 6,000-square-foot customer service center was built, and the firm unfurled new distribution agreements with customers like Kmart, Toys"R"Us, and Wal-Mart.

The Acceleration of Commoditization

Rubbermaid had a great reputation. For fourteen years, it was ranked number one in its industry group by *Fortune* and was named American's Most Admired Company in 1993. Wolfgang Schmitt took over the business two years after Stan Gault retired in 1991. To say that Schmitt, who had worked for the company since 1966, was proud of Rubbermaid would be a gross understatement. An essay by Schmitt in the book *Innovation: Breakthrough Ideas at 3M, DuPont, GE, Pfizer, and Rubbermaid* brims with displays of self-assurance, hubris, and confidence regarding the company's course. Consider the following quotes from the former chief executive officer:

- "Our brands continue to prevail because of our persistent, consistently clever product innovation."[11]
- "Each of our products reflects several generations of innovation, and innovation is what distinguishes Rubbermaid from a sea of competitors."[12]

- "Whatever turns out to be our next breakthrough, I can guarantee that it will reflect changing trends, providing a one-to-one solution for the consumer."[13]

At its peak, Rubbermaid offered 5,000 different items, producing nearly 400 new products each year. A puff piece in *Fortune*, in 1994, credited the firm's creativity to Schmidt's uncanny abilities—he is "thinking, always thinking"—as well as twenty-one development teams consisting of people from marketing, finance, manufacturing, R&D, and sales. The result of these efforts was some truly impressive products, from the heat-resistant spatula (one of Schmidt's ideas) to the Hip Hugger laundry basket.

The Dye Is Cast

In addition to Schmitt's passion for innovation, the company was equally committed to continuing Gault's strategy of selling through the Megas. Explaining the role of the mass discounters to Rubbermaid's future, Schmitt said:

> It's typically the bigger suppliers that can form the sort of close partnerships that retailing's behemoths are increasingly demanding. The goal is to boost sales and reduce costs for both sides by slashing inventories, shortening lead times, and eliminating error: There is a healthy interdependence between us and people like Wal-Mart. We need them; they need us.[14]

The new decade proved to be disastrous for Rubbermaid. As their commitment to the mass marketers increased, so, too, did demands by the Megas for lower prices. At first, Rubbermaid treated pressure from the big-box stores with scorn. For years, they had been able to easily pass along price increases to their distributors who simply charged customers more. However, expectations were rapidly changing.

The ubiquity of Wal-Mart, The Home Depot, Lowe's, and other Megas, coupled with an inflation rate that hung around 2 or 3 percent for most of the decade, had created an expectation that prices would rise only slowly, if at all. Wal-Mart accounted for about 14 percent of Rubbermaid's business when, in 1994, disaster struck.

The key component of Rubbermaid products is polymer-based resins, which make up about one-third of the cost of any given item. The price of resins had been stable for years, but in spring 1994, costs shot up because of new global demand and a supply shortage resulting from problems at key refineries. Within eighteen months, the price of resins nearly doubled, adding $200 million to Rubbermaid's costs.[15] Focused as always on earnings growth, the company increased its prices by what Schmitt claimed averaged, at the most, 6 percent.[16] Rubbermaid's price increases were met with derision by the Megas. The giant retailers objected to monthly price increases and complained that Rubbermaid was unresponsive to the realities of the market. Competitor products were available. Sterilite, a privately held company based in Massachusetts, and Tucker Housewares, a division of Mobil Oil, were ready to fill shelf space at Wal-Mart with much cheaper items. The Megas were ready to jettison Rubbermaid. The problem was termed the "premium gap."

"We let the premium gap get too big in the early Nineties," Schmidt told *Fortune* magazine.[17] The article explained the dilemma this way:

> An experienced householder knows that she should have to pay no more than $10 for a reliable 32-gallon garbage can. When she spots an $8.99 Rubbermaid can next to a competitor's $5 can, Rubbermaid is not concerned. "It's probably thin and breakable, and the customer knows that," says Schmitt. What worries Rubbermaid is a competitor's $7.99 can, because it's probably pretty good. Yet the price is low enough to fall below the 10% premium gap. Thus, Rubbermaid not only loses a sale but may also have convinced the shopper that it is overcharging.[18]

Initially, Schmitt thought that Rubbermaid would be able to weather the resin-based price increase better than his competitors. However, Tucker avoided the resin problem with product designs based on recycled plastics and cedar inserts for storage bins and trashcans. Sterilite was a privately held company that did not share Rubbermaid's aggressive profit goals and was not under the same kind of profit pressure brought to bear by Wall Street.[19]

As the company's innovations became increasingly commoditized, Schmitt attempted to lower costs and increase sales to offset the loss of value. But it was too late. The pressure to create innovative products had often resulted in superficial, cosmetic changes that "created manufacturing complexity and retail confusion" and that resulted in no increase in sales.[20]

The Megas demonstrated only scorn for Rubbermaid, and they reacted with glee as the former wonder company began its downward slide. Said a Kmart official, "Retailers warned Rubbermaid, 'You will kill your business if you don't do something about your prices.'"[21] Another said, "They've been such lousy shippers. Not on time, terrible fill rates, and their products cost too much. They show you a new product line and then tell you they can ship only a third of what you want."[22] Wal-Mart, frustrated with the price increases, emptied shelves of Rubbermaid's Little Tikes, and turned the space over to Fisher-Price.[23]

Left with no other real option, Rubbermaid felt compelled to change gears. In 1994, it began to compete aggressively on the basis of price, offering steep discounts to the Megas. Its margins quickly eroded, and cost-cutting measures were enacted, including the elimination of 1,170 jobs and the closure of nine plants. The company purged 6,000 color and size variations and cut the total number of products by 45 percent.[24] These efforts produced only temporary relief. Rubbermaid was acquired by the Newell Corporation in 1998 for $6 billion in stock.

And what of Little Tikes? The problems that afflicted Rubbermaid in the 1990s—slowing demand and high material costs—also challenged Little Tikes. The firm responded with increased R&D, new product displays, and more product launches. When Newell bought out Rubbermaid, Little Tikes began to invest heavily in consumer research, resulting in original products designed to stimulate the imagination of children. The firm also used innovative weather-resistant technology to produce electronic toys that could be left outside. Little Tikes was tenacious in its attempts to innovate its way around challenges posed by its competitors, distributors, and its new owners.

Despite these efforts, sales continued to slide. In 2001, Toys "R"Us, its largest distributor, began cutting back its Little Tikes inventory to increase sales per square foot. In 2005, Little Tikes generated sales of $250 million—$20 million less than in 1989. Ultimately, the Little Tikes name came to be associated with deeply discounted toys sold on the mass market. In 2006, Newell Rubbermaid sold Little Tikes to MGA Entertainment.

Innovation may be necessary, but it is clearly not enough.

NOTES

1. Justin Scheck and Paul Glader, "Big Companies Invest in R&D to Grab Sales in Recovery," *Wall Street Journal*, April 6, 2009.

2. Ibid.

3. V. Kasturi Rangan, *Transforming Your Go-to-Market Strategy* (Boston: Harvard Business School Press, 2006), p. 38.

4. Paul A. Greenberg, "Cars Online: Miles to Go Before They Sell," *E-Commerce Times*, January 31, 2001, available at http://www.ecommerce times.com/story/7119.html.

5. Available at http://www.ganelyautogroup.com (accessed April 6, 2009).

6. Rangan, *Transforming Your Go-to-Market Strategy*.

7. C. E. Helfat, *Dynamic Capabilities: Understanding Strategic Change in Organizations* (New York: Wiley and Sons, 2007), p. 49.

8. Swasy 1989.

9. Available at http://www.fundinguniverse.com/company-histories/Little-Tikes-Company-Company-History.html.

10. Ibid.

11. Wolfgang Schmitt, "Technology Paves the Way to Perpetual Innovation," in *Innovation, Breakthrough Ideas at 3M, DuPont, GE, Pfizer, and Rubbermaid*, ed. Elizabeth Moss Kanter, John Kao, and Fred Wiersma (New York: HarperCollins, 1997), p. 150.

12. Ibid., p. 151.

13. Ibid., p. 163.

14. Zachary Schiller, Wendy Zellner, Ron Stodghill II, and Mark Maremont. "Clout," *Business Week*, December 21, 1992, available at http://209.85.173.132/search?q=cache:aObXPUcMCKsJ:www.businessweek.com/archives/1992/b329855.arc.htm+%22the+goal+is+to+boost+sales+and+reduce+costs+for+both+sides+by+slashing+inventories%22&cd=1&hl=en&ct=clnk&gl=us.

15. Claudia H. Deutsch, "A Giant Awakens, to Yawns," *New York Times*, December 22, 1996.

16. Tim Carvel and Joe McGowan, "Rubbermaid Goes Thump," *Fortune*, October 2, 1995, available at http://money.cnn.com/magazines/fortune/fortune_archive/1995/10/02/206543/index.htm.

17. Ibid.

18. Ibid.

19. Ibid.

20. Deutsch, "A Giant Awakens, to Yawns."

21. Ibid.

22. Geoffrey Colvin, "How Rubbermaid Managed to Fall from Most Admired to Just Acquired," *Fortune*, November 23, 1998, available at http://money.cnn.com/magazines/fortune/fortune_archive/1998/11/23/251411/index.htm.

23. Constance E. Helfat, Sydney Finkelstein, Will Mitchell, Margaret A. Peteraf, Harbir Singh, Davide J. Teece, and Sidney G. Winter, *Dynamic Capabilities: Understanding Strategic Change in Organizations* (Malden, MA: Blackwell Publishing, 2007).

24. Deutsch, "A Giant Awakens, to Yawns."

Chapter 5

LIVING THE OUTSOURCING COMPULSION

> I don't pay good wages because I have a lot of money; I have
> a lot of money because I pay good wages.
>
> —Robert Bosch

The conventional wisdom in government, business schools, and much of industry is that companies are choosing to close their costly domestic operations in favor of better prospects and profits in other countries. The ability to produce a product for 30 percent to 50 percent less than it would cost at home is widely considered the reason that American firms are flocking overseas. Thus far, the outsourcing (or, more properly, offshoring) conversation has pitted shrinking transaction costs, enhanced efficiencies, and fat profits, against job loss, societal disruption, and a sense of economic angst as industries restructure themselves to conform to the new realities of the digitized age.[*]

Often unrecognized in the outsourcing-offshoring discussion is the strategic dimension. The compulsive embrace of overseas outsourcing—particularly the outsourcing rush, first to Mexico, and then to China—has less to do with international business than it has to do with how products are bought and sold in the

---

[*]This chapter is based on "The Outsourcing Compulsion," by Andrew R. Thomas and Timothy J. Wilkinson, MIT Sloan Management Review, Fall 2006, pp. 10–14, by permission of publisher. Copyright © by Massachusetts Institute of Technology. All rights Reserved.

domestic, American marketplace. The offshoring phenomenon is really about the purposeful weakening of America's industrial structure brought about as a business strategy by the Mega-distributors. The move of American producers overseas is not so much an effort to seek new markets and new opportunities as it is a defensive response to power tactics the Megas employ.

Recent investment in China, for example, has been explained in a number of ways. With 1.3 billion people, it is the world's largest potential market. Firms are rushing in, hoping to capitalize on an emerging middle class of 290 million consumers. Average manufacturing pay of less than one dollar an hour also makes it an attractive option for firms desiring lower wage rates. Finally, in some industries, China offers distinctive skills and expertise that are superior to those found in the United States. For example, Chinese engineers are on the cutting edge of developing technologies in the wireless chip and software industries, and they display formidable product and logistics skills in auto-part manufacturing.[1]

While these observations are factually correct, they tell only part of the story.

It is a fact that American firms are being pulled overseas by the allure of potential profits and cheap labor. The ability to hire software engineers in India at less than half the cost of their American counterparts and the impressive, though inexpensive, capabilities of China's flexible manufacturing facilities produce a siren-like enchantment to Western managers. However, the vast majority of U.S. companies are also being pushed into China—literally being forced to make huge investments in that country—whether they want to or not. This coercive push is being driven by something more proximate to our domestic environment than the desire for new markets, lower labor costs, or greater efficiencies in sourcing.

The underlying reality is that it is not corporate avarice that is driving large percentages of manufacturing out of the United States, nor is it the desire for the cheapest price on the part of consumers. What is forcing thousands of companies to close U.S. operations and lay off workers is the imbalance in the sales and distribution model described in the previous chapters. The compulsive embrace of offshoring by U.S. firms is not a function of internally generated goals and objectives, but it is, instead, driven by the sheer demands of corporate survival.

FOREIGN DIRECT INVESTMENT

Foreign direct investment (FDI) takes place when a company from one country makes an investment in another. It is distinguished from portfolio investment in that, by definition, FDI involves both ownership and control. Examples of FDI include Honda's construction of an auto factory in Marysville, Ohio, in 1982; McDonald's opening one of its restaurants in Moscow in 1990; and Timken's acquiring roller-bearing manufacturing facilities in Romania in 1997. Each of these was an instance in which the parent company invested in foreign countries to access customers. This "market-seeking" FDI is typically what we see in the United States when firms from abroad build auto plants (for example, Toyota), buy our iconic firms (for example, Anheuser-Busch), or work with American companies on joint-venture projects (for example, Électricité de France and Constellation Energy). The other type of FDI is called "factor seeking FDI." This occurs when firms are in search of factors of production such as raw materials or cheap labor.

When China opened up for business in 1979, Western managers initially thought in terms of the Chinese market. China's 1.3 billion people represented a lot of customers with a lot of pent-up consumer demand. However, the FDI that flows into countries in the early stages of economic development tends to go to infrastructure projects, not consumer products. The Chinese government cherry-picked FDI, bringing in businesses needed for modernization and export-oriented firms. It did not allow foreigners to buy Chinese companies or set up their own subsidiaries. Only joint ventures with Chinese partners were permitted. But if American businesses were unable to take immediate advantage of Chinese markets to produce gross profit, they quickly learned that an abundance of cheap Chinese labor could add to their bottom-line growth. It was not until the 1990s that the Chinese government allowed foreign firms to manufacture and sell consumer products in the domestic market. By that time, the pattern had been set and China was utilized as a manufacturing platform for the purpose of in-country production and offshore sales.

The opening of China in the 1990s could not have come at a better time for the Megas. Information technology, particularly the rapid adoption of the Internet as a means of information sharing, eased difficulties associated overseas manufacturing. The

Megas, encumbered by mature market environments, hypercom-
petition, and unrelenting price pressures, were forced to look at
the efficiency of operations to meet performance expectations.
They were met halfway by their vendors, who had been fixated
on a raft of management theories for twenty years or more.
Instead of thinking about connections between production and
distribution, manufacturers were thinking only about how to
become more efficient.

STRATEGY AS BLUNDER

In the early 1970s, manufacturers began to respond to the exhor-
tations of management theorists who preached a doctrine of business transformation that emphasized resources, capabilities,
innovation, technology, and operational effectiveness. Companies
that had once been in control of all aspects of product development, sales, and service were slowly convinced by "leading" business thinkers to focus exclusively on "core competencies" and to
get rid of everything else. Consequently, big companies began to
divest themselves of activities that were not perceived as "value
adding," while, at the same time, embracing operational para-
digms that emphasized Total Quality Management, Materials
Requirement Planning, Just-In-Time Inventory Control, and Lean
Manufacturing.

Eventually efforts to "stick to the knitting" paid off, and firm
boundaries underwent dramatic changes. Companies that previously had exercised power over their value chains were now outsourcing almost everything except those activities that they
considered to be unique to their bases of sustainable competitive
advantage. With rising pressure from perceived higher-quality
Japanese companies, American manufacturers ended up spinning
off not only business functions unrelated to their core resources
and competencies, but also valuable distribution and sales
capabilities.

Goodyear Revisited

As described in Chapter 3, resources used to support The Goodyear Tire and Rubber Company's highly successful existing U.S.
dealer network, which had taken nearly a century to build and

perfect, were reallocated to operations in the 1990s. With less to work with, Goodyear had little choice but to cannibalize its existing distribution arrangement. Wholesalers were turned into dealers and vice versa. Multiple sales outlets began to appear in towns where there had been one or two exclusive Goodyear dealers for years. Consequently, Goodyear's control over the sales and distribution of its products began to erode.

Contributing to Goodyear's downfall was an infatuation with the management fads of the time. In 1989, the company underwent an organization-wide change effort to adopt the principles of TQM. Like thousands of other firms that embraced TQM, Goodyear's operations, logistics, procurement, and research & development (R&D) were retooled with the goal of making "defect-free" products. Sales and distribution, which had been the lynchpin of Goodyear's success, were relegated to a secondary status because TQM focused almost exclusively on the manufacturing process. Inevitably, cracks began to form between the manufacturing people and individuals working in sales and distribution. Shortly after it began to sell its tires through Sears and Wal-Mart, the firm went from being the largest tire company in the world, with a global network of loyal and faithful dealers and strong brand loyalty, to the manufacturer of essentially a commodity that could be purchased at an ever-growing number of outlets for a lower and lower price.

For the consumers of Goodyear's products, this was a boon. Customers suddenly could have Aquatreads or Eagles mounted on their cars while they shopped at the mall or purchased dry goods at big-box stores. Retailers also benefited. Unlike the old system, the new retail outlets were not exclusive dealers. They placed Goodyear tires on their shelves next to competing brands, and, as a result, could offer more choices to their customers. Additionally, the price of Goodyear tires fell precipitously. With a larger number of outlets now competing for the same customer base, price wars became inevitable.

The only loser in the long run was Goodyear—and its workers. A slow degeneration of the company began. Unable to raise its prices through a compromised distribution network where the lowest prices never seemed low enough, Goodyear was faced with the inevitable: the removal of costly manufacturing centers within the United States. Over the next several years, the company would close twelve plants in the United States in favor of cheaper labor overseas. This was done to compensate for losses resulting from the firm's ill-conceived disbandment of its dealer network. Not surprisingly, Goodyear wants half of its global capacity to be in low-cost countries by 2012.

THE NEW SYSTEM

Recognizing the transformation of the new American manufacturing approach was the genius of Sam Walton. He and a raft of imitators stepped in to fill the power vacuum that the strategy gurus had helped to create. The resulting Megas have driven large swaths of America's manufacturing capacity overseas. Now the vast majority of consumer products are sold, distributed, and controlled by entities other than the actual producers.

In the early 21st century, thousands of U.S. manufacturers have little or no control over the distribution and sales of products in their home market. They do not even have control over the price they can charge for their products. This is evidenced by mandates from Mega-distributors imposing yearly price reductions while, at the same time, insisting that suppliers maintain the same high standards of quality and service.

Wal-Mart's ability to squeeze its vendors is legendary. And no wonder, with 30 percent of the U.S. market for household staples such as toothpaste, shampoo, and paper products, and more than 20 percent of all CD, DVD, and video sales, vendors have no choice but to toe the line. Such market power allows the Mega-distributor to home in on every aspect of a supplier's operation—which products get developed, what they are made of, and how to price them.

Sam Walton had an early interest in sourcing from China, and by the mid-1980s, the company was importing a significant amount of merchandise. Concerned about America's growing trade deficit, he launched the "Bring It Home to the U.S.A." program in 1985. For several years, sourcing from Asia was managed through an organization created by Wal-Mart—the Pacific Resources Export Limited. Walton wanted to buy from American companies, but only if domestic firms could compete with overseas suppliers. It was at about this time that he discovered the single most important key in turning the manufacturer-retailer relationship on its head.

Relationships with vendors had been slugfests. Claude Harris, one of Wal-Mart's executives at the time, recalled this in Walton's aptly entitled book, *Made in America*:

> We used to get in some terrific fights. You have to be just as tough as they are. You can't let them get by with anything because they are going to take care of themselves, and your job is to take care of the customer. I'd threaten Procter & Gamble with not carrying their merchandise, and they'd say, "Oh, you can't get by without carrying our merchandise." And I'd say, "You watch me put it on a side counter, and I'll put Colgate on the endcap at a penny less, and you just watch me."[2]

On a famous fishing trip with the vice president of Procter & Gamble (P&G), a new system was worked out based on information sharing, planning, and systems coordination. Sam Walton said the partnership was:

> a model for many of our other vendor relationships. In our situation today, we are obsessed with quality as well as price, and, as big as we are, the only way we can possibly get that combination is to sit down with our vendors and work out the costs and margins and plan everything together.[3]

In reality, this planning process was a one-way street. Wal-Mart, the largest of the Megas, was able to squeeze its vendors mercilessly. If a particular manufacturer was unable to meet the company's exacting specifications, the Mega would seek out its competitor or easily find a close substitute among the throngs of manufacturers flying into Bentonville week in and week out. After a period of stagnation following Walton's death in 1992, the company expanded its own in-house brands by working through unbranded suppliers in China.[4] Indifference to human rights issues by the Clinton administration, and the entrance of the country into the World Trade Organization in 2001, further legitimized China as the major supplier of products sold at Wal-Mart.

Pressed to lower their prices, Wal-Mart suppliers repeatedly have made the discovery that their only option is to shift production overseas. Lakewood Engineering & Manufacturing Company is a case in point. For years, this electric fan manufacturer sold its twenty-inch box fan for $20. Responding to Wal-Mart's downward price pressure, the company opened a factory in Shenzhen in 2000, where labor costs averaged $0.25 per hour compared with $13 per hour in Chicago. By 2003, the fan was sold at the Mega for $10.

In 2008, employees of Lakewood protested, alongside local labor organizations, the company's decision to close its electric heater operations and move production to China. Wal-Mart buys 80 to 90 percent of the company's heaters. Lakewood claimed that its hands were tied because it was heavily mortgaged to Wells Fargo Bank, which refused to lend it more money. The company's relationship with the Mega resulted in the layoff of 220 workers and the outsourcing of production. Who is making money in this deal? Clearly not the manufacturer.[5]

Lakewood Engineering & Manufacturing is not the exception. Seventy percent of the products sold at Wal-Mart either originate from China or have components manufactured in China. In 2004, Wal-Mart sourced $18 billion in product from 5,000 Chinese manufacturers. If the Mega was a country, it would be America's sixth or seventh largest trading partner.[6]

A *Frontline* documentary on Wal-Mart sums it up:

> By now, many American manufacturers . . . have little choice but to redefine themselves as "branded distributors" for overseas goods. In other words, instead of making their own products, they use their own brand names to market Chinese-made goods to retailers. They eke out profits by outsourcing production and mar- keting that production. The process is virtually the final step in the surrender to what Duke University professor Gary Gereffi calls the Wal-Mart-China "joint venture."[7]

Wal-Mart is not the only company that has gained strategic advantage over U.S. manufacturers. Consider The Home Depot's dealings with American Standard, a firm that employs 16,000 people at sixty-three factories around the world, including two factories in the United States and one in Canada. This company sells more than $700 million in bath and kitchen products to The Home Depot each year. But here's the problem: American Stand- ard makes little money selling through The Home Depot. Because of the distributor's size, American Standard has no other viable distribution channel in which to place many of its products. The Home Depot knows this all too well, and every year it pays less for the same products from American Standard than it did the year before. Confidential sources within the senior management of American Standard have shared that it is only a matter a time before the remaining few Canadian and U.S. plants are closed and relocated to China.

Another example is that of Alcoa, which is in the process of reconfiguring its entire North American production facilities. It has been forced to relocate many of its operations to China and the Russian Federation because DaimlerChrysler, after nearly ten years of R&D, decided that it would pay 45 percent less for the wheels that it had been sourcing from Alcoa. As a result, thousands of U.S. jobs have been lost, factories closed, and technology and machinery transferred to the new plant outside of Tianjin.

The companies described above are not exceptions to the rule; they are merely a few of the most visible examples. In home electronics, medical equipment, chemicals, do-it-yourself, and nearly every other industry imaginable in the United States, Mega-distributors have emerged to dominate the sale and distribution of most products.

As a result of the Megas rush to source from China, other retailers have been forced to follow suit to stay competitive. The mail order catalogue company L.L. Bean was for decades the epitome of Yankee independence and all things American. In the 1990s, it was pressed by the raft of new mail-order companies that had appeared on the scene as well as price pressures from the Megas. By 1998, the company was ready to outsource. Chris McCormick of L.L. Bean said this:

> I don't want to overstate it but we were lagging in our sourcing competencies. I'm guessing 60 to 70 percent of our items were probably sourced in the [United States] then. Maybe a little bit less than that but not much. What the consultants pointed out is that the world had moved offshore. Yes, it would be nice if we could keep sourcing products in the [United States], but, realistically, all those jobs were going offshore anyway. The competencies were leaving this country and, from a competitive standpoint, we really had no choice. The quality, by the way, would be just as good if not better than the [United States]. So we created the sourcing department and gave them marching orders to improve our margins and reduce our costs of goods sold.[8]

In 2000, two years after the outsourcing initiative resulted in $30 million in savings, making it a very good year for the company, McCormick said, "It wasn't so much sales growth that drove the performance of that year, it was improving margins that improved profitability of that year."[9] By 2006, only about 20 percent of its items were produced in the United States.

CHINA

Figure 5.1 portrays American FDI into China by the type of investment. Wholly owned enterprises make up fully 43 percent of FDI.
Until the mid-1990s, foreign firms operating in China were
required to work with a Chinese joint-venture partner. The intent
of the Chinese government was to maximize the opportunity for
the newly freed-up industries of China to learn from their foreign
partners. The name of the game was, and still is, technology transfer. The fear of the Chinese government was that, unless foreign
firms were forced to team up with Chinese partners, the Middle
Kingdom could become little more than an export platform—an as-
sembler of components that were invented and understood only in
the advanced industrial world. Instead, a joint-venture strategy
was pursued, and in the 21st century, Chinese industry is heavily
engaged in R&D and new product development within the context
of a large, but still emerging, economy. Forced joint ventures come
at a cost, however, and what was appealing to the Chinese government was often unappealing to American investors. Intellectual
property infringement, operational and logistical difficulties, and

Figure 5.1 Preferred mode of investment in China by type.
Sources: Adapted from A. T. Kearney, *New Concerns in an Uncertain World*
(2007), and the 2007 A. T. Kearney Foreign Direct Investment Confidence
Index.

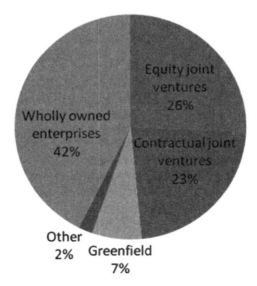

the entire panoply of challenges that accompany large-scale production in cross-cultural settings, served to mute the joint-venture
enthusiasm of U.S. firms.

Contractual joint ventures make up 23 percent of FDI in
China. This is what is taking place when the term "contracting
out" is used. Producers that own and operate overseas factories
tend to lack capacity in the good times, while having excess
capacity in the bad times. The advantage of contract manufacturing over other forms of FDI is that it transforms the fixed-costs
associated with operating a manufacturing plant into a variable-
cost situation. Contract manufacturers are able to keep factories
humming by churning out multiple brands—often of competitors—in
a single factory. This leaves the producer free to focus on marketing,
sales, and design—or so the thinking goes.[10]

Most of the world's desktop and laptop computers are manufactured in China by Taiwanese owned factories. Dell, Hewlett-
Packard, and other producers contract with Hon Hai, ASUSTeK,
Quanta, and others for product assembly and testing. These companies also manufacture consumer electronics and cell phones.
Hon Hai, for example, has a campus in Shenzhen that employs
270,000 people and has net earnings of $2.3 billion.[11]

Liam Casey is an American who operates a company in
Shenzhen called PCH China Solutions. The purpose of the company is to match foreign firms that want to sell specific products
with Chinese manufacturers who are capable of making those
products. Casey says that he is "helping innovators leverage the
manufacturing supply chain here in China."[12] Workers in the
area make between $115 to $155 per month, laboring in difficult,
though not necessarily horrible, conditions.

Perhaps the most famous contract manufacturer is Flextronics,
the industry leader for contracted design and manufacturing of
automotive, computing, consumer digital, industrial, infrastructure,
medical, and mobile devices. Its Web site boasts:

> Starting with product concepts, product design, manufacturing, mate-
> rials management, logistics, reverse logistics and full customer sup-
> port, Consumer Digital meets customer needs in the most efficient,
> cost-effective manner possible. No competitor provides end-to-end
> services across a broad range of consumer digital products. The Con-
> sumer Digital Segment allows OEM and retail brand customers to
> focus on their end users while extending the breadth and depth of
> their brand.[13]

Chief Executive Officer Michael Marks, who took over the company in 1994, had the vision of creating a business in the image of Ford's River Rouge complex with a strategy of vertical integration that could handle the entire supply chain as well the logistics of distribution. As of 2009, the company has more than 100 locations worldwide, and designs, engineers, and supplies products for numerous consumer product firms. It has produced the various iterations of Microsoft's Xbox video game consoles, phones for Ericsson, and disposable cameras for Kodak. In 2006, the fourth-largest toy maker in the world, the LEGO Group, turned production of its little attachable rectangles, triangles, and squares over to Flextronics. These components are now manufactured in Mexico. Production activities in Connecticut, Denmark, and the Czech Republic have been phased out. Flextronics is just one of many companies that facilitate the outsourcing compulsion.

THE NORTH AMERICAN FREE TRADE AGREEMENT

China is not the only destination for firms compelled to outsource production. Mexico has long been a destination for American companies desiring to lower costs by moving manufacturing out of the United States. In 1965, American and Mexican entrepreneurs began establishing factories along the northern border of Mexico. Known as *maquiladoras*, these production facilities operated outside Mexico's stilted policy of import substitution. The system was ingenious. Companies north of the border shipped components to Mexico, where assembly subsequently took place at the *maquiladoras*. The finished products were then exported to the United States for sale to American businesses and consumers. Few, if any, tariffs were placed on the component parts in Mexico, and only tariffs related to value added after assembly occurred on the U.S. side. The program was expanded in 1971 with the passage of a law increasing the *maquiladora* zone along the border and coast, allowing 100 percent foreign ownership; permitting duty-free import of raw materials, machinery, and supplies; and allowing foreign technicians to work at the factories. Over the next thirty years the *maquiladoras* concept was expanded, and Mexico became a primary destination for American companies wishing to lower assembly costs. Only densely populated urban areas like Mexico City and Monterrey were excluded from this arrangement. The key reason for the influx of

U.S. operations into Mexico was the low labor costs. From 1965 to 1996, Mexico managed to stay competitive as an outsourcing destination by periodically devaluing its currency. For example, in 1976 the peso fell by 19 percent with a 32 percent drop the following year.

The North American Free Trade Agreement (NAFTA) that went into effect in January 1994 further opened up Mexico as a platform for reimportation into the United States. It is a mistake to view NAFTA strictly as a trade agreement. While it was sold to the public as a way to open up Mexico to American products, the clear intent was to expand the advantages that the *maquilas* had provided U.S. firms. NAFTA was a resource-seeking trade agreement that conditioned Americans to the idea of moving productive capacity to foreign countries as a means of lowering labor costs.[14] Figure 5.2 shows American exports to, and imports from, Mexico between 1985 and 2007. The figure shows trade between the two countries increasing in tandem for the ten years preceding the implementation of NAFTA. Then in 1995, Mexican exports to the United States outpace American exports, and the gap only widens year by year.

American manufacturers outsource to China and Mexico to access cheap labor. But there the similarity ends. The outsourcing compulsion that forces so many firms into the hands of Chinese contract manufacturers is not as apparent in the context of NAFTA. General Electric, for example, manufacturers everything from electric meters to refrigerators in thirty-five Mexican factories that are managed in cooperation with joint-venture partners. While consumer goods are produced in Mexico, it is the "made in China" label that is ubiquitous in the big-box stores.

A comparison of Mexican and Chinese imports to the United States is instructive. The largest category for both countries is electric machinery, including sound equipment, television equipment, and so on. Both countries also export boilers, machinery, and parts to the United States, as well as furniture, lamps, and other housewares. Of the latter, Mexico exports about $5.5 billion, whereas China exports four times that amount. Apparel and accessories, footwear and parts, and toys and games are among the seven major categories of Chinese imports to the United States that do not appear on the list of major imports from Mexico. China manufactures more than $10 billion worth of toys, puzzles, scale models, and so on for U.S. consumers each year, whereas Mexico exports about one-fiftieth of the same items to the United States.[15]

Figure 5.2 U.S., China, and Mexico trade balances.
Sources: U.S. Census, http://www.census.gov/foreign-trade/balance/
c2010.html#1991, and the United Nations Conference on Trade and
Development.

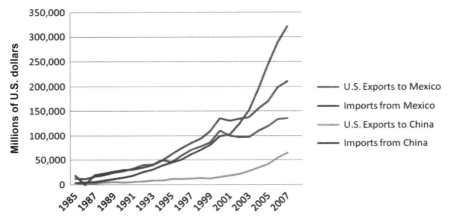

While trade with Mexico is a fraction of what it is with China,
the importance of NAFTA is that it coached numerous American
manufacturers in how to effectively manage resource-seeking
FDI. By the time the Megas linked there information systems with
vendors in the 1990s and began to aggressively press for lower
prices, suppliers knew instinctively that the answer to lower costs
lied overseas. By disaggregating production activities or abandon-
ing manufacturing altogether, it was still possible to make a profit
while serving the needs of the Megas.

In 2003, imports from China exceeded those from Mexico for
the first time (see Figure 5.2). In 2007, the United States
imported $100 billion more from China than it did from the Mex-
ico. China had truly become America's factory.

THE OUTSOURCING COMPULSION

Presently, far too many U.S. manufacturers view outsourcing
overseas as their only option when it comes to "growing" their
business. They are locked out of opportunities at home because of
abnormal relationships with Mega-distributors that not only control the delivery of their products to consumers, but also wield

tremendous power over their internal processes. Cut off from the ability to control distribution and sales, these firms can grow only by cutting costs at the other end of the value chain. They must chase the cheapest inputs, particularly labor, to generate adequate margins and maintain shareholder value.

Equally debilitating is the fact that many of the efforts manufacturers make to invest overseas fail miserably. Because they feel compelled to relocate some or all of their operations offshore, they may not accurately assess the inherent risks in doing business in less developed countries. In China, for example, an overwhelmed infrastructure, competition for scarcer and scarcer resources, a government that frequently protects local interests over those of foreign firms, and an impending currency correction are critical elements that manufacturers often do not, or seemingly cannot, consider. Such factors must be heavily weighed when looking at overseas locations. However, the perils of doing business in emerging markets are often glossed over as the demands of the Mega-distributors compel manufacturers to embrace what appears to be their only strategic option.

NOTES

1. Pankaj Ghemawat and Thomas Hou, "Tomorrow's Global Giants: Not the Usual Suspects," *Harvard Business Review* (November 2008): 80–85.

2. Sam Walton, *Made in America* (New York: Bantam Books, 1993), p. 236.

3. Ibid., p. 238.

4. Sam Hornblower, "Wal-Mart and China: A Joint Venture," Frontline, available at http://www.pbs.org/wgbh/pages/frontline/shows/walmart/secrets/wmchina.html.

5. Anonymous, "Local 1101 Members Rally for Jobs and Severance at Lakewood Engineering," available at www.ueunion.ord/upd_prnews.html?news=393.

6. Thomas L. Friedman, *The World Is Flat* (New York: Farrar, Straus and Giroux, 2005).

7. Hornblower, "Wal-Mart and China."

8. Leon Gorman, *L.L. Bean: The Making of an American Icon* (Boston: Harvard Business School Press, 2006), p. 253.

9. Ibid., p. 264.

10. Kerry A. Dolan and Andrew Tanzer, "Meeting the Makers," *Forbes* 167, no. 10 (2001), available at http://www.forbes.com/global/2001/0430/028.html.

11. Ghemawat and Hout, "Tomorrow's Global Giants."

12. James Fallows, "China Makes, the World Takes," *The Atlantic*, July/August 2007, available at http://www.theatlantic.com/doc/200707/shenzhen/3.

13. Available at www.flextronics.com/en/MarketSegments/Consumer-Digital/tabid/80/Default.aspx.

14. Lance Eliot Brouthers, John P. McCray, and Timothy J. Wilkinson, "Maquiladoras: From Entrepreneurial Experimentation to Global Competitiveness," *Business Horizons* 42, no. 2 (1999): 37–45.

15. Trade statistics are available at export.gov.

Part II

Avoiding the Trap

Criticism simply for the sake of criticism is the purview of only a select few. Those who critique books, movies, plays, and restaurants, for example, do so knowing full well that the veracity of their criticism goes only as far as their personal tastes.

In business, such an approach to criticism is anathema. If someone seeks to disparage a particular business strategy or tactic, they should have a viable alternative. If they do not, then they better step aside.

If the Distribution Trap has taught us anything, it is that much of the current thinking on distribution is gravely flawed. Part I of this book was our attempt at criticism of the actions taken by so many business leaders who abrogate the control of the distribution of their innovations to the Megas.

In Part II of this book we show how a company can stay out of the Distribution Trap in the first place. We begin by looking at how one company, in particular, has experienced great success with a distribution strategy that purposefully shuns the Megas.

Chapter 6

THE STIHL STORY

Things are not always what they seem; the first appearance deceives many; the intelligence of a few perceives what has been carefully hidden.

—Phaedrus, Roman poet

Fred Whyte, president of the U.S.-based STIHL Inc., speaks about the outdoor power equipment produced by STIHL with the same kind of care and deliberation you would expect from someone who was clearing trees with one of the firm's legendary chainsaws. He has been with the company for thirty-eight years—the last eighteen as president for U.S. operations. Before that, he was the president of STIHL Canada for ten years. Whyte remains a Canadian citizen, a fact concealed by a Midwestern accent that avoids even the occasional "eh." When we met with him, we started with this question: "Was there ever a moment that you were tempted to sell through the big-box stores?" He paused for a moment and then followed with an emphatic, "Unequivocally, no." And then he said, "You can't be all things to all people. You have to know who you are and what you are going to be when you grow up."[1]

In the United States, STIHL Inc. markets its products through twelve regional distributors and 8,000 servicing dealers, more than 50 percent of which sell only STIHL-branded handheld products. You cannot buy STIHL chainsaws, blowers, trimmers, or brushcutters at Lowe's, The Home Depot, or Wal-Mart. This is not because there have not been huge efforts to get STIHL products into the Megas. Sales presentations have been made, performance standards have been guaranteed, and huge profits have been projected.

However, the efforts to strike a deal have been undertaken by the Megas—not STIHL. "For quite a period of time, we had Lowe's and The Home Depot representatives flying in here on their private planes, sitting down with us, doing their PowerPoints."

The story of STIHL is a story of invention, creativity, and quality coupled with service, loyalty, and vision. It is the last of these, a remarkable clarity of vision, that has kept the firm out of the Distribution Trap. The company has simply never given the mass-market discounters even one moment of serious consideration. This vision and intelligence, which pervades the company, was instilled by the firm's founder from the very beginning.

ORIGINS

Andreas Stihl liked to figure things out, to know how things worked. Born in Zurich in 1896, and raised by relatives in Germany, he was sent to the front lines in World War II, where he received severe injuries leading to a medical discharge in 1917. With his military service behind him, he studied mechanical engineering at the Technical Institute in Eisenach and spent three years working for large companies, one of which built steam engines for sawmills. It was during this time that he perceived a problem and began to formulate a solution that would revolutionize the forest products industry throughout the world.

The problem he identified was that trees had to be brought down by stationary saws or axes and then transported whole to the sawmills before being cut up into manageable pieces. This involved moving heavy timber over many miles. Working out of a small workshop, Stihl designed and built the first-ever electric chainsaw in 1926—a two-man 140-pound "cross-cutting chain saw." In 1929, he introduced the company's first gasoline-powered chain saw. Although it also required two men for operation, its portability revolutionized the wood products industry.

It was at this time that a particular aspect of Stihl's personality would ensure decades of postwar success and ultimately would protect the company from the Mega-distributors: Stihl truly believed in serving the customer. Employees were trained to instruct buyers in how to use and maintain their purchases. In addition, the company insisted that whoever sold STIHL products had to have the ability to service and repair those products.

One early employee stated, "It won't do to sell saws to people without teaching, assisting and offering good service to users later."

Like any innovation, the chain saw had its share of critics. Loggers, afraid the new technology would put them out of work, vigorously opposed the new technology and even attacked STIHL's salesmen. Stihl dealt with opposition through education and training. In 1937, he confronted the opposition by introducing chain-saw training courses at logging camps throughout Germany, and in a trip to the United States in 1939, he conducted seminars in power-saw technology. These efforts were used to overcome resistance and to introduce potential customers to his revolutionary new product.

Chain-saw training was a lengthy affair that is difficult for us to imagine today. A history written for the company provides the following account from 1939:

> The inhabitants of health resort Langenbrand near Bad Liebenzell in the Black Forest were very surprised when about ten chain saws spluttered to life in the yard of Hotel Ochsen. It was a feast for the eyes of the instructors to see how the district foresters with their chief fellers and forest workers practiced starting the chain saws and sometimes opened the throttle far more than necessary. There were one or two very funny incidents during the first exercise, i.e., starting and cross-cutting, which showed the men were really children at heart.
>
> From the second day of the course, the participants sang their way into the woods where they were able to practice felling and bucking as long as they wanted. In this process, some of the men were so enthusiastic that they forgot that their colleagues also wanted to try out the machines and learn something.
>
> The chief forester in charge, who came into the woods every day on horseback with his head held high, took the course participants under his wing and looked after them. The course continued with lectures, explanations, and practical work until its successful conclusion was celebrated in a festive mood on Friday evening. Chief state forester Evers and Mr. Stihl, with several gentlemen from the company, joined them and the foundation for more chain saw training courses was laid while talking shop, telling jokes, and drinking beer. It should be mentioned that two pigs were slaughtered to provide food aplenty for all. Saturday after lunch, the course participants proudly and happily set off home with new energy and the machines they had bought.[2]

During this time, Stihl continued to improve his saw, creating a lighter weight and more reliable product.

Allied bombing raids during World War II destroyed the STIHL manufacturing facilities in Bad Cannstatt, and production was relocated to Waiblingen. In 1945, Stihl was arrested by French troops and turned over to the Americans. Like all of Europe, the company languished during the immediate postwar period, but by 1948, Stihl was released from custody and eventually returned to the helm of his company.

The major breakthrough for the company occurred in 1950, when STIHL introduced the first one-man saw. An improved version introduced in 1954, at thirty-one pounds, was the first chain saw that was truly portable. New versions followed, including the Contra introduced in 1959 (with its direct drive and diaphragm carburetor) and a saw with an antivibration system in 1965. Constant improvement and innovation characterized the company's products throughout this period.

STIHL's innovations stimulated demand for chain saws, and between 1963 and 1965 output doubled from 65,000 to 130,000 saws. By this time, the business had 50 percent of the German market share and a 16 percent share worldwide. Within a decade, the company's 2,000 employees were producing 340,000 saws annually.

Andreas Stihl died in 1973 at the age of seventy-six. Despite two world wars, raging inflation, crippling poverty, tough competition, and many other obstacles, the inventive mechanical engineer had managed to build a company with 2,500 employees producing the world's leading brand of chain saw. The following year, STIHL opened a 20,000-square-foot warehouse in Virginia Beach operated by fifty employees to facilitate its exports into the U.S. market. By 1960, Stihl's four children had become limited partners in the company, and because of careful planning, the transition to new leadership went smoothly. Hans Peter Stihl was designated as the successor to Andreas in 1972. The company weathered the economic slump of the 1970s and the global recession of the early 1980s. In 1986, it began to offer complementary products, including safety glasses, gloves, boots, helmets, and hearing protectors. New products were also introduced, including trimmers and leaf blowers, as well as specialized clearing saws.

Until the 1990s, STIHL produced chain saws strictly for professional use in the forest and lumber industry. This left 50 percent of the market untouched by the company. Ongoing innovations, including design innovations that reduced the weight of the product to twenty pounds, prompted the company to move aggressively into the small saw market. In 1994, STIHL shifted the production of all small saws to the United States, and, as of 2009, the Virginia Beach operation consists of a more than 1 million-square-foot manufacturing and administrative facility with more than 2,000 employees. In 1973, another manufacturing facility was established in Brazil. A sales office was set up in China in 1995, followed by manufacturing operations in 2005.

STIHL became the market leader in the chain saw segment in 1992, eclipsing both Homelite and the McCulloch Corporation. The STIHL Group employs more than 11,000 people around the world. In addition to chain saws, it manufactures grass and hedge trimmers, leaf blowers, mini cultivators, and other related products.

In a 2008 speech given to employees of one of its American regional distributors, Bryan Equipment Sales in Loveland, Ohio, Hans Peter Stihl attributed the success of the company to four strategies.

First, product innovation and quality. This is the lifeblood of any manufacturing concern. This is especially true for STIHL because of the high expectations our customers have for our products. Whether it is the introduction of new engine technologies that lead our industry by meeting or exceeding strict Environmental Protection Agency emissions standards, or the advanced manufacturing processes that you will find in our Virginia Beach facilities, our customers ultimately experience dynamic products and features that are the hallmark of our brand.

Second, the high level of in-house production. Unlike many other companies, we have not increased our outsourcing of component manufacturing. Actually, we have taken additional processes in-house to maximize quality while minimizing material cost increases and achieving delivery deadlines.

Third, establishing an international manufacturing network. As you are aware, products produced at STIHL Incorporated are distributed across North America and shipped to 126 customers in 85 different countries around the world. Half of the annual production at Virginia Beach is for the export market and STIHL Incorporated can be proud of its achievements in this regard.

Fourth, and perhaps most importantly, the success of STIHL is based on unique marketing strategies. Virtually all of our primary competitors have compromised their retail distribution strategies to accommodate mass merchants, home centers, and the Internet. While this approach may offer some near-term advantages by way of increased sales distribution, the long-term effect can be a loss of identity and competitive uniqueness. This is not the STIHL way. Instead, we rely on our distribution associates, like Bryan Equipment Sales, to build and maintain relationships with our servicing dealers who serve our customers. And, like STIHL, Bryan Equipment is family owned, and I am pleased to now see the third generation of the Bryan family entering into the leadership position within this highly successful organization.[3]

SERVICE

Stihl summed up the company's service philosophy: "These big boxes are not able to give service . . . no service, no sale." Fred Whyte, president of the U.S.-based STIHL Inc., said that STIHL has never been tempted to sell to the Megas because service was a key ingredient of the value proposition from the beginning. "Who likes to buy a new car without driving it around the block?" he asked. "The first challenge for STIHL dealers is to explain why their chain saws may sometimes cost $50 to $100 more than those of competitors." A price-based shopper—and most Americans are fixated on price—will not know that a STIHL chain saw has a unique chain brake, a higher grade chain, an automatic gear-driven oiler, and a chrome-impregnated cylinder with superior heat transfer capabilities and greater durability. A knowledgeable salesperson is required to communicate the superior quality of STIHL products. According to Eric Bolling, the manager of a STIHL dealership in Virginia, a customer will buy a higher-quality product that costs more, "[i]f you can actually show the person what they're paying for."

STIHL dealers "qualify" customers by asking a series of questions so that they can make sure that they get the right product into the customer's hands. They instruct buyers in how to properly use and maintain the equipment they sell, and they offer protective clothing, like chain saw protective chaps, and eye and hearing protectors. STIHL's effort to get protective gear into customers' hands is not just a matter of "plus-selling." Between 2000 and 2004, 32,436 people ended up in emergency rooms as a result of accidents with chain saws. In an article published in the *Wall Street Journal*, reporter Gwendolyn Bounds stated that she

discovered finding critical safety equipment at some big box retailers can be hit or miss. Home Depot and Sears, for example,

carry some eight brands of saws between them, but spokespeople
for both stores say that chaps aren't an item they choose to stock at
this time. Lowe's, by contrast, does stock chaps and offers dedicated
how-to-clinics in regions where chain saws are in high demand.[4]

STIHL dealers also operate full service centers at their retail
stores. The goal is to establish a relationship with customers
while making a "complete sale." By providing a dealer who is an
expert, the customer not only is prepared to properly operate
what can be a dangerous piece of machinery, but also can view
the dealer as the authority when it comes to ancillary products,
whether or not they are produced by STIHL, like lawn mowers,
garden tractors, fertilizers, and so on.

It has never made sense at STIHL for a premium piece of
machinery to be sold in a box without interaction with the customer. For this reason, you cannot buy a STIHL product on the
Internet and have it shipped to your home. STIHL, however, has
shortened the shopping convenience bridge between its dealers
and prospects via its new online shopping program, STIHL
Express. Through this program, a customer can purchase a
STIHL product online and then pick it up at the dealer, who can
provide expert advice and a fully assembled product, fueled and
ready to go. According to the company, selling unassembled products who come in a box, with little or no protective equipment,
and without a reliable dealer who can knowledgably service the
product is the opposite of building a relationship with a customer
and is contrary to the STIHL business model. The nonservice
sales approach ultimately results in low profitability over time.

THE DEALER'S PERSPECTIVE

STIHL believes that its dealers are the lifeblood of the company
and that the most critical point in its distribution channel is "the
three feet of counter space between the servicing dealers and
their customers." For decades, a conscious effort has been made
to help dealers understand that they are a vital part of the firm's
operations. An internal company history records the approach
that STIHL has undertaken with its dealers:

> Groups of dealers from all over the world are regularly invited to
> [the] head office, "so that we could show them our factory and they

could see how STIHL saws are made," explains Reinhold Guhl. In the evenings, Andreas Stihl, while he is still healthy, as well as Hans Peter Stihl, the export boss, and a number of other staff sit down with the dealers to talk things over in a relaxed atmosphere.

Two things are very important at the meetings, stresses Guhl. First, it is necessary to keep underscoring the company's loyalty to servicing dealers because many of them fear that STIHL, as it grows in size, might terminate their agreements at some time. After all, the main competitors switched from specialist dealers to the big chains during the eighties and thereafter.

Second, the photo session is an important part of the meeting with independent dealers. Everyone has a photograph taken with Stihl senior or junior, or both. The pictures are meticulously set up by the company's photographers, with warm hand shakes and friendly smiles all round.

Such pictures are soon hanging on the walls of showrooms all over the world. And dealers point out proudly: "As you can see, I know Mr. Stihl personally. I visited the place where the STIHL saws are built." And long stories are probably told in many places about the great factory and the pleasant evening spent drinking Swabian wine with "my friends Andreas and Hans Peter" and many others. This very personal approach in taking care of independent dealers is largely responsible for the good reputation of the company and the Stihl family among servicing dealers.[5]

STIHL dealers are nearly uniform in their praise of the company. Billings Hardware sits at the far end of Grand Avenue in Billings, Montana. If you walk in the front door and make an immediate turn to the left, you will see a huge display of STIHL products. Dan Thomas, a soft-spoken, articulate man who looks like he is in his mid-fifties, is in charge of service at the store. "I've been in outdoor power equipment since 1979, and I've owned two dealerships of my own. I've worked at almost every level—including manufacturer's representative, service technician, sales, and management. I've done everything there is to do in this industry." Between fielding phone calls, Thomas explained that the industry has changed dramatically since he was in business with his father in the 1980s. "A lot of manufacturers were enticed by big chains and big box stores to increase their numbers as far as sales go. That changed the industry—probably forever. A lot of manufacturers did not survive."[6]

One consequence of manufacturers moving toward the big-box stores was that they lost their relationships with independent dealers. The dealers could not compete with the price points offered by the Megas, so they discontinued the product lines that had been introduced in the big-box stores and sought out high-end manufacturers. Without the independent dealers, no one was around to service or repair units that had been sold. Thomas pointed out that there are exceptions. In Billings, Husqvarna equipment, which is sold at Lowe's, can be serviced at some Big R stores. But if you buy a Homelite or Poulan chain saw, "You are on your own." For purchasers, product reliability is a hit-or-miss proposition. Thomas described the quality issue in this way:

> The outdoor power equipment that's carried in big chains is generally not as good or as high quality as that carried by the independent dealer. That's strictly because the mass merchants want to market something at a lower price. Before the mass merchants became pre-dominant in power equipment, most of the manufacturers had some good products. Once the manufacturers started getting into great big numbers, their quality went down for two reasons. First, they had to produce more units much more quickly. Second, the retail outlets were demanding a much less expensive unit so they put less quality into it and cut corners in their manufacturing. At least as far as chain saws go, [Names 3 brands] were all fairly decent manufacturers back before that huge change in the industry. All of those units in this market are now of lower quality and are sold on the basis of price.

STIHL is viewed positively by Thomas. He stated that the company has a very good brand name and a high-quality product that is "the best quality machine on the market right now." Husqvarna and ECHO are two other nationally known brands that Thomas considers to be "the next best machines." However, when they are purchased at the Megas, customers may or may not end up with a product that is appropriate for a particular job. Thomas explained his approach:

> The first thing I want to do is ask the customer what he is going to use the unit for and how he is going to use it. The worst thing you can do is sell somebody a piece of equipment that's not heavy duty enough to do the job. He simply will not get satisfaction out of that machine. That is true for every line of equipment that is sold. You must get the customer to buy the unit that he wants to use in a certain application.

Thomas has the highest level of technical training offered by STIHL, which he acquired at the company's manufacturing facility in

Virginia. He observed, "Big box stores generally do not have qualified sales people on the floor that can help customers. There are
some individuals who have some knowledge in those places, but not
very many."

An entry on Arboristsite.com is representative of the perspective of many dealers.

> You can tell who's busy at this time of year and who's not. Those
> who are busy are using or repairing their saws. The others whine.
> I was a STIHL dealer for 17 years in a suburban county near
> Washington, DC. I sold my shop a little over a year ago to my
> service manager who's 20 years younger than me. No regrets—I
> loved the business and had great staff, but 3 growing boys made it
> difficult to continue to put in 14 hour days—and often much more
> during the busy season. I had a great relationship with STIHL.
> STIHL is a big company—individual dealers don't buy parts from
> STIHL. Dealers buy parts and whole goods from their regional
> distributor. My distributor was Mid-Atlantic STIHL in Hillsbor-
> ough NC. Never have I dealt with a finer organization—their cus-
> tomer service was excellent and their parts fill rate was even
> better. . . . STIHL does not have a policy that says a part or piece
> of equipment must sell for a certain price. That's price fixing and
> it's illegal. End of story. STIHL suggests a retail price—that
> allows a dealer to make a certain amount of profit—but a dealer
> is free to sell for more or less. I always sold parts and whole
> goods for retail price (certain exceptions were made for high vol-
> ume sales customers). Dealer profit is essential—otherwise there
> won't be any dealers. STIHL also has NO MINIMUM ORDER pol-
> icies. There are incentives such as a minimum size order (it used
> to be $2,500 but may be higher now) to get free freight. Many
> times, a customer needed a part RFN—STIHL would ship it that
> same day and I'd sell it and pass along the freight. Customer and
> dealer happy.[7]

AVOIDING THE DISTRIBUTION TRAP

Peter Burton, STIHL Inc.'s vice president of marketing and sales,
said, "The category killers are tempting. It's easy to get caught up
in the adrenaline rush when they come calling. The kind of volume they say they can deliver, it's huge." The mass-discounter
temptation is tempered by STIHL's vision of its place in the market and by an awareness of what happens to companies when
they do business with the Megas. The downward spiral caused by

the Distribution Trap is well understood at STIHL. President Whyte presented it as a kind of parable:

> The big box store people say, "Andrew you are our most important supplier, a great guy, and we love you to death, and this is a fantastic product you have been giving us." So what does Andrew do? He goes home, sits down with his wife and says, honey, I added The Home Depot account, we're on easy street now, we're going to buy that new boat, and we get to buy the bigger house, and we get the Mercedes. Andrew then hires 20 people, and builds a new building. The second year Andrew comes back and sits down with Home Depot, and the same scenario is repeated, "Andrew, you're one of our preeminent suppliers, but we are going to have to double our volume with you this year with such a successful product." Andrew goes home, sits down with the wife. He gets a bigger boat, he buys a bigger house, he hires more people, he obtains more machinery, he buys bigger buildings. The third year Andrew sits down with Home Depot, "Andrew we've had a great relationship, we love you to death, but this guy Terry Kelley, representing this Chinese company, can sell us this same product for half the price." Now, what is Andrew going to do? Andrew doesn't go home and tell his wife he's selling the boat and laying people off. No, he looks at his chain saw and says, well, you know, we don't have to put chrome on that chain, we don't have to put ball bearings in the engines, we could put in bushings, instead. We don't need a gear-driven automatic oiler, we can put in one that takes a little pressure off the crank case that's manual. And those anti-vibration mounts, well we can just put a bushing in there too. So over time, the quality of the product becomes eroded to meet a price, then you know what happens to the brand after that.

Whyte's parable is not idle talk. He watched it unfold with his company's once-great competitors. McCulloch Motors Corporation, founded in 1943, produced chain saws that were lighter than STIHL's through an assembly-line process that was, at the time, more advanced than the German firm. Renamed McCulloch Corporation, it began to sell through JCPenney in the 1970s and was subsequently acquired by Black&Decker in 1988. Black&Decker had also pursued the mass market, and so diminished their brand image in the eyes of professional contractors, such that they had to reinvent their brand with the launching of DeWALT in 1992.

As of 2009, McCulloch is owned by Jenn Feng Industrial Co. Ltd., a Taiwanese organization, as well as the Swedish AB Electrolux group. Jenn Feng paid a mere $7.5 million for its share of the company in 1999, in part because McCulloch had stopped supplying tools two years before, and its market share had been taken over by the competition. David Jong, the chief executive officer of the Jenn Feng Group, said that the company's initial strategy was to use the McCulloch brand to market its portfolio of lawn care products through The Home Depot, Kmart, Lowe's, and Sears. He said that when they first acquired the company they thought that America's huge retailers would help them quickly boost market share. That did not happen, and McCulloch's share remained small even after two years of aggressively pushing the brand to the Megas. Why did the strategy fail? Jong explained it this way:

> You can't count on huge retailers to help you realize your dream because they have so many suppliers and usually pick a few big players as their long-term sources. If you are not one of their favored suppliers, they only buy in small quantities from you, and when your products sell out, you often find that the shelf space has been given over to the products of your rivals. Most of all, they shop for price, so there is constant pressure to discount. Or they import products from your rivals.[8]

In 2003, Jenn Feng stopped dealing with the Megas, and, instead, according to Jong, intended to focus on supplying gas engines for handheld garden tools for U.S.-based MTD Products Inc. In 2008, Jenn Feng was acquired by Husqvarna.

A similar fate befell Homelite, which, when it was a division of Textron, ramped up sales on the mass market. By 1978, it had sold 1 million chain saws in a twelve-month period. The company was sold to John Deere in 1994 and sold again in 2001 to the Hong Kong firm Techtronics after losing $70 million in 2000 and $30 million in the first nine months of 2001. Ken Golden, the public relations manager at the time, stated, "Despite the very best efforts of many employees, Homelite has not been profitable."[9] Homelite chain saws are now available only at The Home Depot. The Homelite Web site prominently features a product recall required by the Consumer Product Safety Commission. If you Google Homelite you will be bombarded with consumer complaints and recall information.

Speaking to business students at Northwestern's Kellogg School of Management, STIHL Inc.'s vice president of sales and marketing, Burton, summarized the problem with the Megas:

The big boxes are . . . intimidating. They dictate guarantees and shift costly operational activities off their own backs and onto suppliers. And they expect their suppliers not just to hold down their prices but to consistently drop them annually. In short, the supplier is left helpless and increasingly profitless. If you sleep beside the 8,000-pound gorilla, you don't want to be caught underneath when it rolls over.[10]

The management of STIHL views selling to the Megas as a "vicious circle." Firms are forced to lower their prices to be competitive and then reduce costs to remain profitable, which in turn leads to diminished product quality, and, ultimately, a brand that has been tarnished, sometimes irreparably. Hans Peter Stihl stated, "We remain true to our distribution philosophy of selling exclusively through servicing dealers because mass merchandisers are not in a position to provide optimal advice and handle technical service and parts support."[11]

THE ADVERTISING CAMPAIGN

STIHL not only eschews the Megas, but also lets the world know about it. Over the past few years, it has paid big money to place some very provocative ads in the *Wall Street Journal*, *USA Today*, *New York Times*, and other national, regional, and local newspapers. A picture of a STIHL chain saw sits under the caption, "Why is the world's number one selling brand of chain saw not sold at Lowe's or The Home Depot?" Another ad reads, "Why is it that some Father's Day gifts can't be found in a big box?" Explanations of the service and maintenance aspects follow in smaller print. The ads were intended not only to reinforce the "aura of exclusivity" that surrounds STIHL products, but also to educate potential buyers about where they might find STIHL products. Research conducted by STIHL had indicated that more than 50 percent of survey respondents thought that the company's products could be purchased at Lowe's and The Home Depot. Whyte explained, "Generation X and Generation Y visit Home Depot and expect to be able to find everything there." Indeed, the local gas station has disappeared from small-town America as has the corner grocery store. The appliance stores that used to be front and center in small-town America have been replaced with the likes of tattoo parlors, T-shirt shops, and boutiques specializing in hemp. The younger generations, having no memory of

Figure 6.1 STIHL ads.

local, specialty stores, think that everything can be found in the big-box stores. STIHL's advertising campaign has been aimed at undermining this misperception.

The impetus behind the *Journal* ads actually came from the company's dealers, who began to constantly challenge the corporation's stated commitment to sell only through the dealer service network. The thinking was simple: everybody sells through The Home Depot, so of course STIHL would eventually sell there as

Why is the world's number one selling brand of chain saw not sold at Lowe's or The Home Depot?

We can give you 8,000 reasons, our legion of independent STIHL dealers nationwide. We count on them every day and so can you. To give you a product demonstration, straight talk and genuine advice about STIHL products. To offer fast and expert on-site service. And to stand behind every product they carry, always fully assembled. You see, we won't sell you a chain saw in a box, not even in a big one. **Are you ready for a STIHL?**

Go to: www.learn-why.com or call 1-800 GO STIHL.

The Home Depot and Lowe's are registered trademarks of their respective companies.

Number 1 Worldwide **STIHL**®

well. The idea for full-page ads came to Fred Whyte over a beer with Peter Burton. "We decided that we were going to put our dedication to our service dealers in print. We swallowed really hard, but we knew it was the right thing to do." Hans Peter Stihl liked the idea, "You can put it in print," he said, "as long as I own the company, we will only sell to servicing dealers."

STIHL's marketing efforts have engendered tremendous enthusiasm from the dealer network. The campaign caused a stir when the ads initially appeared in the *Wall Street Journal*. When asked about the ads, The Home Depot spokesperson, Jean Osta Niemi, said, "Those vendors who are selling their product at The Home Depot realize the benefit of 2,060 store locations and 1.3 billion customer transactions a year, and they, too, are committed to providing the best product at the best value." Ravjiv Lal, a Harvard Business School professor who specialized in retailing, was paraphrased in the same article as saying that it was a risky strategy because it implied that consumers who shop at big-box stores do not appreciate quality. "You can offend a bunch of people," he said, "but those probably aren't your customers anyway." STIHL has become enormously successful by ignoring this kind of "insight" while sticking to its core vision of customer service.[12]

SEEKING OUT NEW RETAILERS

STIHL has not spurned all of the companies who have approached them. In July 2008, the manufacturer reached an agreement with John Deere, which made it the preferred provider of handheld power equipment at Deere dealers across the United States and Canada. Executives at STIHL "thought long and hard" when John Deere informed them that it had decided to exit the handheld market. Deere proposed that STIHL become the preferred brand of handheld products offered through Deere's network of dealers. "It was the first time a non-green product went into the Deere stores with the blessing of their corporate office," said Whyte.

> They are a very well-recognized, international brand. They were obviously going to sell some kind of handheld product, so it was pretty amazing when they came to us and said, "look, we have exited the handheld market, and you guys have been so successful that we want you to fill the void."

The complementary nature of the products sold through John Deere makes this distribution arrangement particularly attractive. Deere sells a variety of consumer and professional lawn and garden products, as well as tractors and heavy equipment used on farms and ranches, and STIHL does not compete with John Deere in any product category since Deere exited the handheld category.[13]

While the deal with John Deere expands the reach of STIHL, distributing through suppliers of farm and power equipment is still somewhat limiting. Many people simply do not place themselves in that kind of environment. One of the reasons that The Home Depot and Lowe's have been so successful is that they reinvented the hardware store and lumber yard categories. For many people, going to the lumber yard or hardware store was a less-than-pleasant shopping experience. Employees who were great at cutting boards and mixing paint were often socially ill equipped to deal with people who did not know much about fixing things. Such customers often felt foolish in the lumber yard environment. As much as anything, this created the multi-billion-dollar do-it-yourself home improvement category. STIHL executives recognize that many potential customers simply will not walk into the metallic atmosphere of a tractor or power equipment store. This, plus the proliferation of mass discounters, has pushed STIHL to continually search for new distribution opportunities that fit with its service and maintenance philosophy.

STIHL executives see hardware stores as a natural outlet for its products. Whyte especially likes Ace, Do it Best, and True Value.

They are good business people, generally located in metropolitan areas, on nice pieces of real estate. They are open longer hours, whereas our traditional retailer is not open on Sunday and closes at six o'clock during the week. These stores are convenient. Ace, True Value, and Do it Best people are pretty sophisticated. They have shown their retailers that the average sale per square foot for STIHL products is something like 10 times what they are accustomed to in their stores. This is because they are selling a premium product. Even though they have access through their national buying programs for items made by Poulan and Weed Eater, the hardware owner also wants to be able to offer a premium product. We added dozens of Ace dealers in the last year. That is some very significant business. Again, the point is to segment potential customers—the customer who is more comfortable in that retail environment than going into a power equipment shop or even a John Deere dealership.

STIHL continues to look for opportunities to expand its distribution throughout North America and around the world. It is amenable to evaluating options when it comes to getting its products into the hands of customers. However, it is uninterested in the Megas or in branding the products to be sold under a different name. In the early 1990s, STIHL acquired Viking, a European company started in 1984 that manufactures lawn mowers and garden equipment. You will not buy one of these lawn mowers in the United States because 80 percent of the walk-behind lawn mowers are sold through the big boxes. STIHL refuses to allow its products to become commoditized, even when those products are sold under a completely different brand name.

Recently, as Whyte got on a plane after attending a trade conference in San Diego, the chief executive of a well-known national brand that competes with STIHL turned to him and said, "Well, the good news is that I'm on my way to Atlanta to see my biggest customer, and the bad news is that I'm on my way to Atlanta to see my biggest customer." Because STIHL is determined to control the destiny of its products, its executives do not have to face this good-news, bad-news scenario.

NOTES

1. All quotes from the president of STIHL Inc., Fred Whyte, come from an interview on February 10, 2009.

2. Waldemar Schäfer, *STIHL: From an Idea to a World Brand* (Stuttgart: Schäffer-Poeschel Verlag, 2006), p. 26.

3. Speech by Hans Peter Stihl, Bryan Equipment Sales, Loveland, Ohio, 2008.

4. Gwendolyn Bounds, "Did It Myself: Joining the Chain Saw Gang," *Wall Street Journal*, February 4, 2006.

5. Schäfer, *STIHL*, p. 91.

6. Interview with Dan Thomas, Billings Hardware, February 23, 2009.

7. Available at http://www.arboristsite.com/showthread.php?p=1394127.

8. Cen.com. "Interview with David Jong, ECO Jenn Feng Group," July 11, 2003.

9. "Deere & Co. Abandons Homelite Line," *American Nurseryman*, October 15, 2001.

10. All quotes from Peter Burton come from "Thinking Outside the Box Stores: Stihl VP Talks Channel Strategy with Kellogg Students," February 13, 2008, available at www.kellogg.northwestern.edu/New?Articles/2008/peterburton.aspx.

11. "What Is Your Special Formula for Success, Mr. Stihl?" *Blick Ins Werk*, no. 1 (2007), available at http://www.stihlusa.com/MrStihl75/HPS_interview.pdf.

12. Timothy Aeppel, "Too Good for Lowe's and Home Depot?" *Wall Street Journal*, July 24, 2006.

13. Information about the John Deere–STIHL deal was obtained from: "John Deere and STIHL Announce Agreement to Expand Retail Relationships" (STIHL press release), July 29, 2008; and "John Deere & STIHL Reach Handheld Equipment Deal," August 2008, available at www.landscapemanagement.net.

Chapter 7

CONTROLLING YOUR CHANNELS

Defeat has its lessons as well as victory.
—Patrick J. Buchanan

The challenge (and risk) of distributing innovations through channels that do not encroach on the innovators' fair share of the profits is particularly acute for small to mid-size businesses as they attempt to scale up and become larger enterprises. The allure of the mass-market draws scores of small producers to Bentonville each day in the quest for Wal-Mart's access to millions of customers. To successfully select and manage distribution, managers must have a thorough understanding of the power structure that determines the winners and losers in channel relationships. By doing so, strategies can be developed to decide on appropriate channels and, in rare instances, successfully manage relationships with the Megas.

Channel power is the inverse of dependence. A manufacturing company's power decreases to the extent that it needs a Mega to push its products into the market. For either producers or distributors, power can be measured through proxy indicators, including sales and profits provided and performance in the channel compared with competing firms. Figure 7.1 illustrates the factors that compose the producer-distributor power structure.

Figure 7.1 Power structure.
Source: Adapted from V. Kasturi Rangan, *Transforming Your Go-to-Market Strategy* (Boston: Harvard Business School Press, 2006), p. 100.

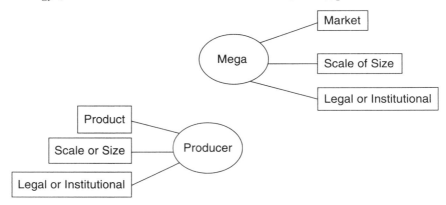

SOURCES OF POWER FOR THE MEGAS

Scale

The most obvious, and perhaps the most determinative variable in the power structure, is the comparative scale of the producer and the distributor. Historically, big companies (with a few notable exceptions) have been able to dictate terms to retailers. With the rise of the Megas, few producers are in a position to stand on equal footing. As has been pointed out, not only are the large retailers able to cut into the margins of the producing company through systematic and forced renegotiations over pricing, but they also are able to shift the cost of traditional retailing activities onto manufacturers.

One of the most effective methods of managing suppliers is through what are called "category captains." Large retailers have learned that they can maximize their advantage by selecting a major supplier to manage a category of products—including those of competitors—so that the category maximizes the Mega's profitability. A category captain typically manages the merchandising of an aisle or a section of the store and provides the retailer with information on category sales and trends, planning and merchandising advice, and suggestions for shelf space allotment. The captain's ideas are only recommendations, but they are taken seriously by retailers who cannot possibly have the same level of expertise as the category captain. Because category captains manage products other than those they produce, they must work closely with competitors. As Barry C. Lynn put it in an article in *Harpers*:

> One obvious result is that a producer like Colgate-Palmolive will end up working intensively with firms it formerly competed with, such as Crest manufacturer P&G, to find the mix of products that will allow Wal-Mart to earn the most it can from its shelf space. If Wal-Mart discovers that a supplier promotes its own product at the expense of Wal-Mart's revenue, the retailer may name a new captain in its stead.[1]

Clearly, size and scale have their privileges, especially for distributors.

Markets

Megas have power over producers because of access to consumers. They have the ability to reach customers of almost all economic and demographic profiles in numerous markets. This is what motivates producers of all sizes to sell through the large distributors. PenAgain, for example, is a small company that manufactures a uniquely designed ergonomic pen for the mass market. After selling the pen through independent distributors for a number of years, firm founders Colin Roche and Bobby Ronsee were eventually able to distribute through Fred Meyer stores and Hobby Lobby, and, after an intense sales effort, through Wal-Mart. Soon Walgreens was on board along with Office Depot and others. As a result, PenAgain now has market-reach far beyond what would have been possible if the company had stuck with its independent distributors and online sales. Naturally, serving the mass market-means turning a large degree of control over to the Megas, and PenAgain has been forced to outsource production to China, produce lower-priced products, and come up with financing to support the orders of its big retail clients.[2]

Large firms are also drawn to the Megas because of the market power that the big retailers exhibit. Levi's, Goodyear, Procter & Gamble (P&G), and the other firms discussed in this book all altered major components of their respective value chains so that they could sell through the mass discounters. The reach of the large-scale distributors is phenomenal, and their ability to capitalize on that reach is breathtaking.

Legal Context

The legal and regulatory environment places constraints on the relationships formed between producers and the Megas. Because power was concentrated in the hands of producers for so many years, the legal environment eventually shifted so that, in the early 21st century, it now favors distributors. A modest shift back toward manufacturers has only recently taken place.

One of the most obvious (and detrimental) placements of regulatory power is in the automobile industry where the Automobile Dealers Day in Court Act of 1956, and subsequent franchise laws, made it nearly impossible for the automakers to manage how their cars were sold. The act reads as follows:

> An automobile dealer may bring suit against any automobile manufacturer engaged in commerce, in any district court of the United States, in the district in which said manufacturer resides, or is found, or has an agent, without respect to the amount in controversy, and shall recover the damages by him sustained and the cost of suit by reason of the failure of said automobile manufacturer from and after August 8, 1965, to act in good faith in performing or complying with any of the terms or provisions of the franchise, or in terminating, cancelling, or not renewing the franchise with said dealer. Provided, that in any such suit the manufacturer shall not be barred from asserting in defense of any such action the failure of the dealer to act in good faith.[3]

A 2006 article in the *New Yorker* describes the impact of the act:

> Car dealers, with their low-production-value TV commercials and glad-handing tactics, seem like the archetypal small businessmen, and it's hard to believe that they could sway the decisions of global corporations like G.M. and Ford. But, collectively, they have enormous leverage. Dealers are not employees of the car companies— they own local franchises, which, in every state, are protected by so-called "franchise laws." These laws do things like restrict G.M.'s freedom to open a new Cadillac dealership a few miles away from an old one. More important, they also make it nearly impossible for an auto manufacturer to simply shut down a dealership. If G.M. decided to get rid of Pontiac and Buick, it couldn't just go to those dealers and say, "Nice doing business with you." It would have to get them to agree to close up shop, which in practice would mean buying them out. When, a few years ago, G.M. actually did

eliminate one of its brands, Oldsmobile, it had to shell out around a billion dollars to pay dealers off—and it still ended up defending itself in court against myriad lawsuits. As a result, dropping a brand may very well cost more than it saves, since it's the dealers who end up with a hefty chunk of the intended savings.[4]

The American automakers are squeezed on both ends; unsustainably high union-enforced labor outlays coupled with huge legacy costs on one end, and a dealer-instigated stranglehold on the distribution of automobiles on the other. Defenders of the dealerships argued that dealer proliferation was irrelevant to General Motors Corporation (GMC) because the dealers operated as independent businesses, purchasing cars and paying for their own operations. Said one letter published in the *Wall Street Journal*, "So what if a dealership sells only 100 units a year? Each is a sale on which the manufacturer gets a monetary return."[5] However, an article published in the *Denver Post* on June 2, 2009, one day after GMC filed for bankruptcy, explained how the dealers helped to kill the company:

> For years, critics of the company called for the elimination of the Oldsmobile division and the GMC truck division, which sold clonal [*sic*] versions of Chevy trucks. But GM found itself handcuffed to its obstreperous network of dealers who were protected by state franchise laws. It cost GM more than $1 billion to buy out Oldsmobile dealers when, at last, the division was closed in 2004.[6]

As GMC plunged into bankruptcy and announced the closure of hundreds of dealerships, national and state politicians cried foul, demanding that the government step in and save the dealerships. Even after the goose was dead, the politicians were demanding that it keep on laying golden eggs.

Often people complain that the Justice Department does not pursue antitrust violations with the Megas like they have done with manufacturers like Microsoft, or service companies like Google. However, the antitrust laws are set up to prevent firms from acting in a monopolistic fashion, for the ultimate purpose of increasing prices. The Megas, with their low-cost strategy and penchant for driving down prices, are not violating the antitrust laws. Their business model, with its focus on low prices, does not act against the best interests of consumers. While the Federal Trade Commission has shown some interest in the area, calls for breaking up monopolistic retailers have been largely ignored.

Another example of how the Megas have used laws and regulations to their advantage can be seen in their use of private-
labeled products. These offerings have been a great boon for the
Megas. In category after category, large retailers have outsourced
the production of copy-cat brands or knockoff products and have
placed them on their shelves right next to branded products. The
most audacious example of private-label offerings is Wal-Mart's
poaching of the White Cloud line of toilet paper, previously
owned by P&G. The consumer products manufacturer, having
decided to focus on Charmin, let its trademark for White Cloud
expire in 1994. Wal-Mart acquired the rights to license the brand
from the company that picked it up after discovering P&G's
lapse.

Other pickups, while not as obvious, have been every bit as
successful and have been protected by the courts. *Trade dress* is a
legal term for the nonfunctional characteristics of a package or a
product, including design elements. The boxes containing Apple
Computer, Inc.'s products, the packaging used for Wonder Bread,
or the Happy Meal box used by McDonald's are examples of trade
dress. The U.S. Supreme Court has ruled that trade dress is not
necessarily protected by U.S. trademark law. Circumstances
prompting the court's decision are explained in a ruling in which
Wal-Mart prevailed over a garment company that had sued for
trademark infringement:

> Petitioner Wal-Mart Stores, Inc., is one of the nation's best known
> retailers, selling among other things children's clothing. In 1995,
> Wal-Mart contracted with one of its suppliers, Judy-Philippine, Inc.,
> to manufacture a line of children's outfits for sale in the 1996 spring/
> summer season. Wal-Mart sent Judy-Philippine photographs of a
> number of garments from Samara's line, on which Judy-Philippine's
> garments were to be based; Judy-Philippine duly copied, with only
> minor modifications, 16 of Samara's garments, many of which con-
> tained copyrighted elements. In 1996, Wal-Mart briskly sold the so-
> called knockoffs, generating more than $1.15 million in gross profits.[7]

Wal-Mart's victory means that producers must now be able to
prove that buyers perceive trade dress to be a marker of the company's branded products. If a company has not documented the
connection between *trade dress* and its brand, much of what the
company considers the brand can be copied legally and sold by
its retail partner.

POWER OF PRODUCERS

Figure 7.1 also displays the power that producers have in their dealings with distributors. While sources of manufacturer power mirror that of distributors, the ability of producers to wield countervailing power equal to that of the Megas is becoming increasingly rare.

Product

The greatest source of power that a company has when dealing with distributors is its products. Firms that sell truly differentiated innovations may be able to successfully distribute through the Megas during the early phase of the product life cycle. A true innovation requires market space in which there are few, if any, real competitors and sufficient lead time, created either by patents, brand power, market reach, or some other delimiter that keeps competitors at bay. Once technological, legal, or operational vulnerabilities weaken an innovation's market position, the once-vaunted product can easily become just another brand sitting on the shelf next to a private-label version sold for half the price. In fact, marketing though the Megas almost ensures the unraveling of a product's power in the marketplace.

Mass-market distribution necessarily places a barrier between the manufacturer and the customer. While this does not matter for products that are already commodities, it makes a big difference for innovative products. For many companies, selling through the Megas removes the ability to effectively offer service and repair work. Defective products are sold and then returned to the Mega without any opportunity on the part of the manufacturer to interact with the customer. The likelihood that products that require servicing will be properly maintained is greatly reduced. This reflects poorly on the producer, not on the distributor. Moreover, many products sold through the Megas require assembly by the purchaser, which often frustrates customers and further alienates them from the manufacturer.

Distributing through the Megas also robs the manufacturer of the opportunity to sell appropriate ancillary items. "Plus-selling" is left to sales associates who are unlikely to know about complementary products offered by the producer. For example, a John

Deere riding mower can be outfitted with five variations of a "cargo mount" (for example, electric spreader, oscillating fan), eight different kinds of bags, and four different types of snow blowers. It is unlikely that a sales associate at The Home Depot or Lowe's would have the knowledge to guide a customer through these various options even if all of these choices were available.

Scale or Size

Large manufacturers with well-known, sought-after products, have the best potential of going toe-to-toe with the Megas. A Harvard Business School case described how P&G employee Tom Muccio moved to Bentonville to manage the company's relationship with Wal-Mart. The two sides have been able to work together to overcome various challenges and disputes over the years. For example, it cost P&G $0.90 to sell a unit of Pampers to Wal-Mart for $1.00, which Wal-Mart wanted to sell for $0.83—a $0.17 loss per unit. This conflict was resolved by providing the retailer with a second, large-size unit priced more favorably along with other joint efforts designed to increase sales. These efforts resulted in an increase in inventory turnover from twenty to seventy-five times annually. What is clear from the case is that not only have the two sides been able to negotiate as partners rather than as adversaries, but also P&G has benefited from its relationship with Wal-Mart. The bottom line is that P&G is simply too big to push around. Fifteen percent of the company's sales are to Wal-Mart, making both parties vulnerable to any vagaries in the relationship.[8]

   In contrast, another Harvard Business School case disclosed that the real key to working with Wal-Mart is to understand its culture and to be able to communicate concerns in a way that is understood by its buyers. One of the key negotiation principles at the end of the case pretty much sums up the position of the smaller company "negotiating" with Wal-Mart: "Don't spend time griping. Be problem solvers, instead. Approach Wal-Mart by saying, 'Let's work together and drive costs down and produce it so much cheaper you don't have to replace me, because if you work with me, I could do it better.'" Doesn't that sound just great?[9]

Legal or Institutional

A number of legal protections afforded to producers can help manufacturers protect themselves from encroachment by the Megas. A U.S. Supreme Court ruling in 2006 reinterpreted the Sherman Antitrust Act so that suppliers could prohibit retailers from advertising prices below what was authorized by the producing firm. This policy of a minimum advertised price (MAP) is intended to protect a brand's image from being harmed through discounting practices. Typically, MAP programs are tied into the producers' advertising policies so that retailers forgo advertising reimbursement from vendors if they advertised a price below the one that has been authorized. MAP assists producers in two ways. First, it helps to protect smaller stores from price-based advertising carried out by the Megas. To bypass the major discounters and sell through independent distributors and specialty stores, smaller outlets have to exist. MAP helps to level the playing field by making comparison shopping more difficult. Second, even though manufacturers cannot legally control the price charged by retailers, prohibitions against advertising a cheap price lessens the risk that the brand will deteriorate under a withering assault of big-store discounting. Commoditization of the brand is still likely for other reasons (for example, displaying quality products next to cheap knockoffs), and consumers are beginning to understand the MAP concept and are adjusting their shopping behavior accordingly. Plus, the ability of the Megas to offer unadvertised discounts to customers remains unimpeded. This means that companies that sell through the Megas may be compromising other channels in which a discounted price is not an option.[10]

Perhaps the most important legal protection that individual producers enjoy is patent protection. However, as pointed out in the discussion of trade dress, patents can take you only so far. While the liability of the Megas increases as they "work with" manufacturers on the production of low-end products, designing around patents is a normal practice and is encouraged by antitrust law as a way to spur innovation. Sometimes the Megas do not go far enough in their efforts to produce something that can stand up in court; at others times, they get it just right.

Manufacturers have successfully used institutional power in a broad array of circumstances. Efforts by auto manufacturers to persuade the U.S. government to limit Japanese imports

during the 1980s, the Banana War of the 1990s, and protection-
ist measures against foreign steel during the first terms of
George W. Bush all represent industry's ability to push Washing-
ton into helping American commercial interests. In contrast,
manufacturers have yet to see the Megas as a threat to entire
industries. Because the Megas are viewed simply as another link
in the supply chain of the U.S. economy, manufacturers have
not used their trade associations or other political platforms to
alter the rules that govern their relationships with the mass-market
discounters.

DISTRIBUTION STRATEGY

There is a right answer for how firms should distribute their
products. The optimal solution exists, but it is different depending
on the industry in which a company operates. If you are the chief
executive officer (CEO) of a behemoth company, like P&G or
General Electric, you may do just fine dealing with the Megas.
But if you are merely the CEO of a giant company, like Goodyear
or Rubbermaid, you may want to explore other options in distributing your products.

We believe that many American businesses should create
superior value by producing high-quality products and then
bypass the Megas to get those goods into the hands of customers.
Taking a product to market with the intention of avoiding the
mass market may mean slower growth in the short run, but it will
translate into greater profitability, satisfaction, and freedom—yes,
freedom—over the long term.

Directly to the Customer

In some circumstances, the best way for a firm to fully exploit an
innovation is to sell directly to customers. As tools like customer
relationship management software, database management programs, and Web-based customer service become more affordable
to businesses of all sizes, the possibility of directly targeting a
company's micromarket comes well within reach. The benefits of
customer intimacy, loyalty, and word-of-mouth advertising that
are achievable with effective direct marketing should make it a
top consideration in efforts to avoid the trap of losing control over
innovated products.

David Oreck, the founder of the Oreck Corporation, purposely eschews the Megas in favor of dealing directly with customers. He strongly advocates that businesses create and sell premium-priced products while avoiding mass-market channels. According to Oreck, "Any manufacturer who does not control distribution will eventually be controlled by the distribution channel."[11] Oreck sells his vacuum cleaners online and through company-owned and franchise stores. Direct marketing, especially online selling, requires a lot of advertising to direct people to a Web site or an 800 number. Oreck has masterfully personalized his product through extensive television and radio advertising.

Drawbacks to Direct Marketing

While direct marketing has proven to be a great strategy for many companies, avoiding intermediaries has a number of disadvantages. First, high advertising costs are the major drawback in direct marketing. Television commercials, direct mail, and tele-marketing are expensive ventures. Even an online presence requires massive advertising for customers to become aware of, and interested in, particular products. The online dating service, eHarmony, for example, spent an initial sum of $3 million in radio and television advertising to launch its brand. As of 2009, it has about 4.9 million "visitors" and brings in around $200 million a year. From 2005 to 2008, eHarmony rival Match.com spent $180 million on promotions but barely increased its paid subscribers— from 1.2 million to only 1.3 million.[12]

Second, direct marketing can be a problem if the augmented product requires a high degree of service. In Chapter 8, we discussed STIHL's insistence that its chain saws be sold only in conjunction with customer training and maintenance and repair capabilities. As we pointed out, STIHL does not sell its products online but only through authorized servicing dealers.

Third, in some instances, direct marketing may hinder the potential growth of the company. David Dyson's bagless vacuum was developed at great cost of time and money. But it was unique and it caught on in the United States, Japan, and Europe. It had sales of £514.7 million in 2006, 30 percent of which were in the United States. Although the Dyson was initially sold in specialty stores, versions of the product were eventually distributed through the Megas. This product is currently the top-selling vacuum cleaner in America. The market share achieved by Dyson would not have happened had the company limited itself to direct marketing. An excellent product, incredible brand power, huge market share, and a carefully fashioned strategy that aggressively maintains and enforces patents have permitted David Dyson to successfully deal with the Megas.[13]

Dealers

Manufacturers often employ regional distributors responsible for developing local dealerships, which then sell products directly to the public. Distributors frequently provide training, logistics, and marketing and sales support for these dealerships. For companies with high-end products, especially those requiring a service component, authorized dealerships may be the best way to distribute the product and retain value from the transaction. Specialty stores, whether operating as chains or as independents, are still found across the United States. Many companies that now sell through the Megas at one time sold only through authorized dealers. Firms like Rubbermaid, Goodyear, Little Tikes, Levi Strauss, Harry London Candies, McCulloch, and Vlasic Pickles made their fortunes by working through extensive dealer networks and distributors. Other companies, like STIHL Inc., have avoided the Distribution Trap and have operated through dealerships for their entire existences.

Aluminum siding was invented by Alside in 1947. Several years later, the company became a leading innovator in vinyl siding and windows, with a broad array of patents and cutting-edge technology. Former president and chief operating officer Donald Kaufman primarily used authorized dealers to distribute the company's products. He said, "If we had a good distributor in a local market, we wouldn't distribute the product in-house." Kaufman described the relationship between the company and its dealers as one of "mutual dependency." The goal of Alside was for its dealers to view themselves as partners rather than as customers. The company provided its local distributors with a wide range of products, inventory management control systems, and sales and product specific training.

Alside kept is distributors on board through a combination of carrots and sticks. In a 2008 interview, Kaufman explained Alside's approach:

The key with distributors is they must also be a partner...not just a customer. Distributors were almost always given an exclusive area in which to operate. He needed us as much as we needed him. We ran dealer incentive trips, which were expensive. The goal was to keep the customer on board. Distributors were given points for performance. When they earned enough points, they could go on a trip. Trips were pretty important. One of the advantages of trips was that you couldn't go unless your bill was current. The final cut for the trips would take place twice a year with no carry over for the points. This motivated people to keep current on their bills. We kept pushing authority down to the distributors so that the local guy could make decisions. We also had quotas that were fairly negotiated with distributors. No sense in setting it too high. We did it by quarters. What I needed was the ability to walk away. At the end of two years, each side was able to terminate with a 90 days notice.[14]

Drawbacks to Dealers and Distributors

Working with distributors means that the company must be willing to invest in the development and organization of numerous independent dealerships. This can be accomplished through a distributor-to-dealer arrangement, as in the case of STIHL, or directly from the corporation to the independent dealer-distributor, as in the case of Alside. In either case, potential partners must be sought out, qualified, trained, and then incentivized. Managing hundreds of distributors and dealerships is much more complicated than managing just a few large accounts. This is undoubtedly one of the major reasons that so many companies have been drawn into the Distribution Trap. Controlling distribution is a costly and difficult undertaking. Managing a business, including distribution channels, is work.

Owning Stores

One obvious way to bypass the Megas is to vertically integrate and sell your product through company-owned stores. Typically, this is done in combination with other forms of distribution. In addition to its independent distributors, Alside operates ninety of its own outlets. This provides the firm with flexibility in terms of entering new markets or pressuring its independents to do a better job. In addition to its online presence, Oreck's primary mode of distribution is through its stores. In recent years, well-known manufacturers have opened stores to showcase their products and to control distribution. LEGO operates eighteen "concept stores" so that it can provide room for customers to play with its 240 bins worth of bits and pieces uninhibited by the shelf space limitations imposed by the Megas. Similarly, Bose, Nike, Puma, Lacoste, and Harley-Davison manage their own retail outlets.[15]

The operation of retail stores can be undertaken to showcase items, as in the instance of LEGO, or as the major method of distribution, as in the case of Harley-Davison and Oreck.

Drawbacks to Owning Stores

Retail is a tough business. Operating a chain of stores requires an entirely different set of skills than does product development and manufacturing. For technologically based companies, the advantages afforded by store operations may dissipate as the needs of customers change. Gateway Computers, for example, had a successful chain of computer stores that offered computer classes and attentive support for its many customers. However, as people became familiar with computers, the need for such attention lessened. The value proposition changed. The company closed its 322 outlets in 2004. Even companies that have a great deal of expertise in merchandising are reluctant to go into the retail business. Leon Gorman, the chairman and former president of L.L. Bean, was pushed by his colleagues to open stores in the 1980s. Although the company does have retail outlets today, Gorman's initial reaction to retail was anything but positive.

> I opposed retail expansion. I had never seen another retailer that was successful in both retail and catalog. The two channels required different sets of merchandising skills, logistics technology, corporate cultures, and customer services. None of the people advocating retail expansion at L.L. Bean had any experience in retailing, and, I thought, they didn't understand the fundamental differences between the two channels and the challenges of a retail expansion.[16]

Opening stores can also create channel conflict. Independent dealers and distributors do not like to compete with their suppliers' stores. Manufacturers that pursue the retail route must make it advantageous to their distributors or risk losing their business. This may involve creating different products for each channel, creating enforceable rules of engagement, and compensating the parties that participate in a sale regardless of which business makes the actual transaction. One study noted that channel conflict can be handled if "the supplier acts as an administrator, steering the parties in different directions, giving them different means of engaging the prospect, and compensating the victims of intertype competition."[17] That's a big "if."

USING THE MEGAS

Perhaps the only company that has perfected *the store* as a way of leveraging the Megas for its own purposes is Apple Computer, Inc. For years, Apple struggled under the shadow of the software behemoth, Microsoft. In 2001, the company reinvented itself and essentially created a new product category with the launch of the iPod. This product has been sold at Target, Best Buy, Wal-Mart, Amazon.com, and other outlets, including 170 Apple stores. Mass marketing the iPod through the Megas was a departure for Apple, which previously had distributed its products through authorized dealers and a few (failed) distribution attempts through large retailers like Sears and CompUSA. The company opened a series of stores in 2001 to display the entire product line. Apple's 2005 annual report states, "By operating its own stores and building them in desirable high traffic locations, the Company is able to better control the customer retail experience and attract new customers."[18] Why did Apple pursue a mass-market strategy with an innovative new product in the same year that it opened its own outlets out of frustration with the performance of the Megas?

The mass-market launch of the iPod put Apple front and center as America's premier technological innovator. By 2004, the iPod had 92.1 percent of the market for hard-drive-based music players, and, in 2007, it was responsible for 35 percent of the company's revenue.[19] Given the mass-market success of the iPod, it is instructive to note that the iPhone was sold only through the Apple Web site and company-owned stores, along with AT&T's (then called Cingular Wireless) 2,100 stores and Web site. Apple's careful control of distribution allowed it to capture a much larger share of the margins than it had been able to do with the iPod. However, this took place only after the company had developed the "i" brand through the Megas. The iPhone appeared at Wal-Mart stores in late 2008—almost two years after the initial launch of the product. Apple was able to use the Megas to develop its brand through the iPod and then cash in with tight control over the iPhone. The company entered the Distribution Trap and not only avoided getting caught, but also was able to use the Megas to vastly increase its business. Keep in mind, however, that Apple is an exceptional company.

A more typical way of successfully dealing with the Megas was carried out by Alside. Don Kaufman says, "The operators of the big boxes are the worst people to do business with. We wouldn't sell to them because they would deteriorate the brand image. Our customers felt that when they were buying our premium product, they shouldn't be able to find it at Home Depot."[20] However, the company did successfully work with Sears by employing what Kaufman calls the 10 percent rule. No customer was allowed to represent more than 10 percent of the firm's total sales. This simple rule limited the danger of becoming overly reliant on Sears. For many companies, the adoption of such a rule would mean that they could never do business with a Mega because they would be unwilling and unable to gear up adequate production to meet the immense demands of the mass market while keeping sales under 10 percent. Kaufman refused to allow Sears or any other distributor the option of setting a price. He said, "The moment you allow that to happen, the game is over." A company that adopts this rule will be unlikely to do business with the Megas because dictating a price point and then reverse engineering costs to make that price point feasible is *the* modus operandi of the Megas.[21]

OTHER APPROACHES

A number of other approaches to channel strategy hold out the promise that firms can do business with the Megas while avoiding the Distribution Trap. We are skeptical.

Segmenting the marketing according to channel is one such possibility. Here, producers sell different versions of the same product through different distributors. John Deere, for example, sells lawn tractors and various lawn and garden equipment through Lowe's and The Home Depot. The company's lawn tractors are clearly inferior to those sold through John Deere dealerships. Kelly O'Keefe, the executive education director of Virginia

Commonwealth University Adcenter, commented on this approach in an article in *Advertising Age*:

> John Deere has had many complaints about service about its stripped-down line that is in Home Depot stores. Clearly, they compromised quality to reach a broader audience, but they would say they were just expanding to a new market with a new line. I don't know of any examples where the company would agree that they cut quality to save cost.[22]

Evidently, John Deere cut back its quality to extend market reach through the Megas. Such "segmentation" tarnishes the brand. Eventually, the word gets around, and customers become wary of all the products offered by the manufacturer. Two comments on a Web site dedicated to complaining about John Deere lawn tractors illustrate the point (all misspellings *sic*):

> Craig of McVeytown, PA (1/4/09):
> I just read many complaints on John Deere lawn mowers and noticed most were bought at big box stores ie: Lowes and Home Depot, that tells me that what I have always said that the quality of the things that are made for these stores by big name manufactures is lower than that made for there regular stores-dealers. I was a self employed plumber and saw this all the time with faucets and other items and would not go to these places and purchase things for my customers to avoid call backs. As far as J.D. goes I have owned a 425 lawn and garden tractor since 2000 and no complaints and have used it very hard. Only things done to it are normal oil changes and maintenance. I will only buy John Deere lawn equipment and only from there dealers.

> Jay of Catheys Valley, CA (7/10/03):
> In my opinion, John Deere made a big mistake putting their lawn and garden equipment in Home Depot and Sears or any other chain store. I compare that business practice to selling a Cadillac at a GoKart dealership. By doing this, John Deere is cheapening their product and hurting their dealers. John Deere is also cutting the quality on their replacement parts, at least on their lawn and garden equipment which makes me wonder if they are sacrificing quality in other areas of production.[23]

Another example of segmentation through distribution channel is Jones Soda. During the mid-1980s, consumers were hard pressed to find a soda pop made with cane or beet sugar. Because many people are allergic to corn-based products, there is a substantial market for products made without corn syrup. Jones Soda entered this market space with the creation of a line of soft drinks sweetened only with cane sugar. Originally an obscure, specialty product, the firm had successfully segmented its market through its distribution channels. After initial distribution consisting of ice chests in tattoo parlors and snowboarding shops, the firm eventually was able to sell its bottled products at Starbucks, Panera Bread, and Barnes & Noble. In 2005, it made its initial foray into the mass market by entering a two-year distribution deal with Target. It also signed up with National Beverage, increasing its retail reach from 2 percent of the market to up to 50 percent. The deal with National Beverage was largely limited to twelve-ounce cans of Jones Soda and sixteen-ounce energy drinks sold through most of the Mega-distributors. The other dozen or so flavors are sold through 280 distributors. In addition, National Beverage distributed and manufactured Jones Soda products, thereby providing a buffer between the Mega-distributors and the innovative firm. By the time the exclusive deal with Target ended in 2006, Jones Soda showed a profit of $39 million on $406 million in revenue. The company decided to pursue the mass market and compete with Coca-Cola and Pepsi by selling through Wal-Mart, Safeway, and other Megas. A report on CNNMoney.com explained what happened next:

> [I]n 2007, the company posted an $11.6 million loss, created largely by founder Peter van Stolk's attempted expansion into the canned-soda market. The move marked a radical departure for Jones, putting it up against behemoths Coke and Pepsi in mass-market retailers such as ... Wal-Mart. At the end of the year, Jones Soda replaced its founder with Stephen Jones, a former marketing executive at Coca-Cola.[24]

Jones Soda had abandoned its strategy of direct contact with young customers for big deals with the Megas. "'Cans are commodities that many retailers use as loss leaders,' Jones said, 'So we'll [sic] reduce the number of cans we were selling. They were draining cash.'" For many companies, dealing with the Megas is a slippery slope that ends in ruin.[25]

Another suggestion, called *channel stewardship*, is championed by Harvard Professor V. Kasturi Rangan. According to Professor Rangan, a channel steward "considers the channel from the customer's point of view. With that view in mind, the steward then advocates for change among all participants, transforming disparate entities into partners having a common purpose."[26] The idea is that all channel participants become motivated to create a value proposition that is attractive to both consumers and channel members. Stewardship involves constantly directing and guiding changes in managing the channel so that it is aligned with customers' needs while, at the same time, creating profit for all channel participants. Who is this channel steward? Professor Rangan stated that the role can be played by any partner in the channel. "In some cases, the supplier is in a better position, and in other cases, the distributor or retailer is more suited to the role."[27] Professor Rangan pointed to Wal-Mart as an example of both a "channel steward" and a "power monger." The former role is illustrated by the company's relationship with P&G and Coca-Cola. He stated that Wal-Mart's conduct with these companies "exemplifies" the channel stewardship strategy. However, he also pointed out what is really behind Wal-Mart's relative flexibility when dealing with these companies. He wrote, "Without the power of the national brands at everyday low prices... Wal-Mart would lose its appeal to its customers. It is a symbiotic relationship. The brands and Wal-Mart need each other."[28] And what if Wal-Mart doesn't need your brand? After discussing Wal-Mart's takedown of Vlasic Pickles, he stated, "If... that same sale is used to crush its competitors... and unwittingly its own suppliers, then Wal-Mart has destroyed long-term value for its consumers. It is a delicate balance and often not easy to calibrate."[29] We disagree with this conclusion and suggest the real lesson is that most companies should run away from the Megas as fast as they can. There is no such thing as "stewardship" when the other side possesses overwhelming power.

We think that the best alternative is to avoid the Distribution Trap altogether. Distribute your product through channels other than those provided by the Megas. Do not become greedy. If you do, you will likely pay a heavy price for your avarice.

NOTES

1. Barry C. Lynn, "Breaking the Chain: The Anti-Trust Case Against Wal-Mart," *Harper's Magazine*, July 2006, available at http://www.harpers.org/archive/2006/07/0081115.

2. Gwendolyn Bounds, "You Got a Big Break: Now What?" *Wall Street Journal*, November 13, 2006; Gwendolyn Bounds, "Pen Maker's Trial," *Wall Street Journal*, July 18, 2006; Gwendolyn Bounds, "One Month to Make It," *Wall Street Journal*, May 30, 2006; Gwendolyn Bounds, "The Long Road to Wal-Mart," *Wall Street Journal*, September 19, 2005.

3. American Bar Association, *The Franchise and Dealership Termination Handbook* (Chicago: American Bar Association, 2004), p. 275.

4. James Surowiecki, "Dealer's Choice," *The New Yorker*, September 4, 2006, available at http://www.newyorker.com/archive/2006/09/04/060904ta_talk_surowiecki.

5. Jerry Briskin, letter to the editor, "Are Dealers an Asset or a Burden?" *Wall Street Journal*, June 9, 2009.

6. "As GM Goes, So Could the U.S." *Denver Post*, June 2, 2009, p. 6A.

7. *Wal-Mart Stores, Inc. v. Samara Brothers, Inc.* (99–150), 529 U.S. 205 (2000), 165 F.3d 120.

8. James Sebenius and Ellen Knebel, "Tom Muccio: Negotiating the PSG Relationship with Wal-Mart," *HBS Alumni Bulletin*, January 11, 2008.

9. James Sebenius and Ellen Knebel, "Sarah Talley and Frey Farms Produce: Negotiating with Wal-Mart," *HBS Alumni Bulletin*, November 8, 2006.

10. Quentin "Tim" Johnson, "Minimum Advertised Price Program," 2004, available at http://www.frelaw.com/articles/marketing/mark-0401-qtj.html.

11. Bruce Freeman and Diana Layman, "At 82, David Oreck Never Gives Up," Scripps Howard News Service, February 8, 2006, available at http://www.oreck.com/about/press15.cfm.

12. Marissa Miley, "Dating Site Still Attracting Users," *Advertising Age*, 80, no. 8 (2009); Monica Steinisch, "Savvy Shoppers Know 'Minimum Advertised Price' Isn't Always the Bottom Line," May 29, 2009, available at http://hffo.cuna.org/12433/article/1059/html.

13. J. Hall, "Dyson Bags Dividend of £30m," Telegraph.co.uk, March 11, 2007.

14. Interview with Donald Kaufman, former president and CEO of the Alside Corporation, Summer 2008.

15. Paul Sloan, "Why Some Brands Can Stand Alone," *Business 2.0*, October 1, 2005, available at http://money.cnn.com/magazines/business2/business2_archive/2005/10/01/8359257/index.htm.

16. Leon Gorman, *L.L. Bean: The Making of an American Icon* (Boston: Harvard Business School Press, 2006), pp. 147–148.

17. Alberto Vinhas and Erin Anderson, "How Potential Conflict Drives Channel Structure: Concurrent (Direct and Indirect) Channels," *Journal of Marketing Research* 42, no. 4 (2005): 514.

18. ifo AppleStore, "The Stores," available at http://www.ifoapplestore.com/the_stores.html; Bharat N. Anand, "The Value of a Broader Product Portfolio," *Harvard Business Review* (January 2008): 20–22.

19. David Becker, "It's All about the iPod," CNET News, 2004, available at http://news.cnet.com/Its-all-about-the-iPod/2100-1041_3-5406519.html.

20. Interview with Donald Kaufman, former President and CEO of the Alside Corporation, Summer 2008.

21. Ibid.

22. Erik Sherman, "The High Price of Rapid Growth," *AdAge*, August 20, 2007, available at http://www.prophet.com/newsevents/news/story/20070820story.html.

23. Available at http://www.consumeraffairs.com/homeowners/deere.html.

24. Maggie Overfelt, "A Cult Soda Brand Fights for Survival." CNNMoney.com, October 10, 2008.

25. Ibid.; "Jones Soda Company," *Beverage World*, August 16, 2007; "Keep Up with the Jones, Dude!" *Business Week*, October 26, 2005; "Jones Soda Co. and National Beverage Enter into Exclusive Distribution and Manufacturing Agreement" (Jones Soda Co. press release), September 19, 2006; Ryan Underwood, "Jonesing for Soda," *Fast Company*, December 19, 2007; "Panera Inks Distribution Deal with Jones Soda Co.," *St. Louis Business Journal*, June 25, 2003; Dan Burrows, "Soda Maker Should Benefit from Nationwide Rollout," *Smart Money*, March 1, 2007.

26. V. Kasturi Rangan, *Transforming Your Go-to-Market Strategy* (Boston: Harvard Business School Press, 2006), p. 11.

27. Ibid., p. 160.

28. Ibid., p. 159.

29. Ibid.

Chapter 8

USING A DIRECT MARKETING STRATEGY

> A customer is the immediate jewel of our souls. Him we flatter, him we feast, compliment, vote for, and will not contradict.
>
> —Ralph Waldo Emerson

When you envision a product like aluminum siding, it does not stretch one's thought to imagine it being distributed as a commodity where price is the determining factor. In fact, for the layperson, it might be difficult to conjure up anything else. But when you listen to Donald Kaufman talk about the company he ran as chief executive officer (CEO) for a quarter of a century, you can observe clearly the difference between a leader who falls into the Distribution Trap and one who consciously stays out of it.

Jerome Kaufman, Donald's brother, invented baked enamel aluminum siding in 1947—a true innovation. That same year, the company, Alside, was born. In 1960, Alside went public and was listed on the New York Stock Exchange the following year. From the beginning, although the company was viewed primarily as an innovator and manufacturer, it worked equally hard to control the sales and distribution of its products. Fundamental to the business was the direct relationships the firm enjoyed with its customers. For three decades, Alside built and maintained a network of exclusive distributors across the country who worked directly with local contractors to install aluminum siding on millions of American homes.

When Donald Kaufman took over as president and chief operating officer (COO) in 1974, the aluminum siding industry was becoming fractured, with Megas already altering the landscape. The commoditization race appeared to be on. The temptation to Kaufman to cannibalize the Alside distribution network in the coming years was very real. Alside's competitors were already compromising the control over their products to the Megas. It seemed almost inevitable that aluminum siding would go the way of so many other products and become a price-driven commodity, swallowing up firms like Alside in the wake.

In the midst of this storm, Kaufman was faced with one of those so-called defining moments. He could take the easy road and follow the crowd: abrogating control to the Megas while lining his own pockets as Wall Street rewarded the short-term rise in volume. Or, he could dig in and face the threat head on, focusing on the long-term sustainability of the company.

To Kaufman's credit and the resulting success of Alside, he stood firm. He realized who the best customers for Alside were and aligned his needs with theirs. He did it by focusing his company on strategic customers and avoiding the Megas, and by going directly to those important customers and building the kinds of long-term, sustainable, and profitable relationships that all companies need to succeed.

ALIGNING THE NEEDS OF SUPPLIER AND CUSTOMER

At its core, marketing is the direction a company takes to deliver value to the marketplace. When we try to understand marketing in relation to the Distribution Trap, we are ultimately trying to determine whom we really want as our customers.

Customers are not created equal, nor should they be treated the same. Most leaders we talk to seem to understand this at a basic level. Many, however, when faced with the daily rigors of setting and executing strategy in a hypercompetitive global marketplace, often let operational concerns obscure this fact. At times, they tend to treat the biggest customers—also the biggest volume buyers of their products and services—as their best customers. Size seems to matter. Kaufman was aware of this pitfall and constantly reminded his team that it was profitability, not volume, that separated good customers from marginal ones.

The thinking—rooted in volume—goes something like this: "The more that we sell to you, the customer, the more you are valued." As we have discussed, this is where the Trap can begin. It is essential to determine whether, in fact, those big volume customers are really the most profitable ones.

SO HOW DO WE DO IT?

We need to be cognizant that marketing is a two-way street. It involves a relationship between the supplier and the customer. In the mass-marketing paradigm that is characteristic of the Distribution Trap, innovative companies get out of alignment because their relationships become out of balance. The customer becomes dominant and the relationship becomes dysfunctional.

A two-way relationship with a customer that is balanced means that needs are aligned between the two parties. These needs are based are on the criteria of timeliness, loyalty, vision, and, ultimately, profitability.

Typologies of Customers

As shown in Table 8.1, there are three general customer typologies— the Transactional, the Preferred, and the Strategic. Certainly, we could get into more specific areas, but that is not the purpose of this discussion. The purpose is to illustrate the broad scope of categories under which customers can fall.

The Transactionals are the least attractive type of customer. The Preferred are more attractive. The most attractive are the Strategic customers. Strategic customers are the kinds of companies with which we would want to form strong bonds and alliances and that enable us to grow our products and services over time. These Strategic customers enable us to continue to deliver value and to maintain the inherent nature of our innovative products and services.

Assessment Criteria

Implicit in this discussion is the fact that volume is not a determining factor. As we examine the various criteria, note there is no criterion for how much activity exists with a particular customer. As

Table 8.1 Typologies of customers and need assessment.

Criteria	Transactional	Preferred	Strategic
Primary Interest	Price driven	Relationships over products	Long-tem mutual dependence
Time Frame	Short-term or no contracts	Longer-term	Integration of processes and systems
Focus	Focus is on transaction alone	Quality focus	Future (market) driven
Demands	Demands are not justifiable	Demands provide learning opportunities	Demands enhance common possibilities
Relationship Approach	Us versus Them	You and I	Together
Loyalty	Little or no loyalty	Moderately loyal	The most loyal
Profitability	Little profitability	Moderately profitable	The most profitable

Source: Andrew R. Thomas, "An Analysis of Sales and Distribution Strategies of U.S. Firms in Romania," doctoral dissertation, Academia de Estudii Economice, 2007, p. 27.

mentioned earlier, the profitless prosperity that so often exists when companies do business with a Mega permeates a company's performance when we look at it from a volume perspective.

In other words, say we are doing 60, 70, or 80 percent of our business with a Mega—a Wal-Mart, an AutoNation, The Home Depot, or a group of insurance brokers. If we are in the Distribution Trap, an analysis will show that all we are really doing is turning money over. We are not doing a whole lot of anything except maintaining the product or service flow to the Mega.

Primary Interest

Primary interest is the first criteria. Transactional customers are price driven, and if anybody can recollect a time when they have dealt with a Mega, this criterion will be easy to understand. What separates the companies who are able to do business with a Mega from those who cannot is price. Can you deliver on price? And not simply can you deliver on price today, but are you able to meet the constant demands for reduced prices year after year? This is what so many innovative companies fail to realize. It is not simply meeting the Mega's price the first day that you sit down to do business with them, but can you meet their price after the first year, the fifth year, and the tenth year?

As we saw in Chapter 5, that inability to meet those constant demands for lower price—Transaction customers being price driven—is what compels innovators ultimately to offshore and outsource the production of their products and services.

Moving across Table 8.1, you will see Preferred customers as they relate to the primary interest criterion. They *do* value their relationships over products. They are not as price driven as Transactional customers. Price still plays a key role, but it is not the only role, and, certainly, when we get to the highest level of customer, the Strategic, the primary interest is a long-term mutual dependence. They are looking for that two-way street where "we need you as much as you need us."

Time Frame

If you look at the time frame for these customers, the Transactionals are based on the short term. If they do have contracts, they are month to month, quarter to quarter, or year to year, and that is reflected overwhelmingly in price. Preferred customers tend to have a longer-term perspective. The time frame for Strategic customers tends to be much longer, in fact, the longest, because, in this case, an innovation of processes and systems takes place—that is, alignment between supplier and customer. A synergy is being created and it takes time, but that is okay from the point of view of the Strategic customer because time is something they are willing to commit.

Focus

Regarding the focus for the typologies of customers, not surprisingly, the Transactional is focused on the price they want to pay and the amount of product or service that they want to buy. If everything aligns at that particular moment, everything can work out. But, again, everything is based on that one transaction.

The Preferred customers are willing to pay more because they see a value coming from the quality of the product or the service that they are acquiring from their supplier. At the top end, the Strategic customer is not only looking at what profits can be made today, but also at what an enhanced relationship with the supplier might mean over time.

Demands

The demands from the Transactional customers are simply not justifiable. They want everything. They want lower price, better shipping terms, and plenty of credit. But far too often, companies who embrace the mass-marketing paradigm jump whenever asked to do something for a Transactional customer because many times these Transactional customers are by volume the biggest percent of their business. Yet, as we have seen, Transactional customers are not driven by anything except the short-term results and the price. Preferred customers, in looking at their demands, are thinking about a learning opportunity and a possible way to integrate further with their suppliers. At the Strategic level, demands are a way to build common possibilities that strengthen the alignment between the two firms.

Relationship Approach

When you listen to the conversation from a relationship approach, it becomes very focused on "us versus them" on the Transactional level: "We're going to get the lowest price because we need to." It is confrontational, and it is hostile. At the Preferred level, there tends to be more of a coming together, a mutuality of need, and "you and I" are used. At the Strategic level, you hear "together"—not simply today, but into the future as well. "We are going to do this." "We are going to make this happen." This collaboration can take place because of the long-term point of view that each party maintains.

Loyalty

Loyalty is needed in relationships with customers. At the Transactional level, so driven by price and the short term, there is little or no loyalty. A moderate level of loyalty exists in a Preferred relationship. Perhaps it can become more, and if it does, it moves to the Strategic level where the most loyal customers reside.

Profitability

Finally, and most important, we are in business to make profits over the long term and to sustain those profits. Transactional customers, although they may be the biggest group, are not the most profitable. Operational demands and the desire to beat up manufacturers over price, coupled with the negative approach that Transactional customers bring to the relationship, create a situation in which these customers are the least profitable. At the Preferred level, profits will be higher than at the Transactional level, and the Strategic customers are the most profitable.

THE FOUNDATION OF A DIRECT MARKETING STRATEGY

It is important to ask questions when looking at any company in terms of the way they do their marketing: What is the direction that they are taking to bring value to the marketplace? Who are they are doing it for? And how are they doing it? Are they focusing on Strategic customers? Are they building relationships with those Strategic customers that align the two firms? On the other hand, are they focusing primarily on the Transactional level?

Core to this notion of the different kinds of relationships with customers is not simply how the innovative company producing a product or service looks at its customers. Equally important is how those same customers look back at that innovative company.

If you are dealing with Wal-Mart, which has 100,000 plus suppliers, you might ask: How many of those suppliers does Wal-Mart really need? How many of those suppliers would be viewed from a Strategic point of view in Wal-Mart's eyes? There are certainly Strategic suppliers from Wal-Mart's perspective—Coca-Cola, Procter & Gamble, Johnson & Johnson, and maybe a few dozen or a few hundred others.

Wal-Mart views most of its suppliers in a Transactional way. In other words, if it does not get the price that it wants, if it does not get its demands met, and, ultimately, if it cannot make money off those products or services that are purchased, then it simply will cut those suppliers loose. The dysfunctional nature of the Distribution Trap takes over when the supplier, which Wal-Mart may and probably does view as Transactional, puts all or most of its eggs in the Wal-Mart basket—mistakenly believing that Wal-Mart is in fact a Strategic customer.

These days, most Transactional and even some Preferred customer relationships are the result of a mass-marketing approach. Little or no profitability is provided by these customer types. If the Mega gets a better chance for lower prices, they are going to walk away without a thought—without leaving any chance for loyalty to be grown.

An effective marketing vision is about focused, direct relationships with Strategic customers. Of course, it is essential to meet standards of excellence in business, but it must be done at the Strategic level, and, to a lesser extent, the Preferred level.

MAKING SUCCESSFUL DIRECT MARKETING POSSIBLE

Many organizations find the changes in database management and communication technology to be so overwhelming that they do not know where to begin and how to compete. For those who read direct marketing as just another buzzword in an industry that has many buzzwords, it is important to know that direct marketing is not a tactic but rather a strategy. A tactic is a device for accomplishing an end, whereas a strategy is a careful plan or method. In a football game, a trick play is a tactic but a well-rehearsed plan to contain an explosive runner is a strategy. Direct marketing is a careful and well-thought-out plan leading to successful customer interaction. Done properly, direct marketing becomes marketing in every sense of the word, not only for large companies but for small companies as well.

Marketing used to be applied to the masses. When its poor outcomes outdated it, marketing was then aimed at smaller groupings called segments or niches. Direct marketing is aimed at the individual market. The individual market is the Strategic customer. The dentist's office calls to remind you about your appointment. The closest grocery store asks for your card to record your purchases. You turn fifty and receive membership information from AARP. These are all examples of the impact of direct marketing in everyday life. Very quietly and often without much fanfare, the most visible applications of direct marketing have changed the way we go about living, and there is no evidence to suggest that the impact will lessen.

The old Yankee peddler knew his Strategic customers, and in that wagon of his was almost every imaginable thing that frontier families might need. As he traveled, he listened to the people and listed their needs so that perhaps by the next time he came through their town, he might have just what they wanted to make their new dwelling a real home. Marketing has changed in that same direction—more direct, highly focused, and interactive.

With 21st-century technology, knowing and serving the customer is both a step back and a step forward.

The Twelve Steps

To implement a direct marketing strategy, the Taylor Institute for Direct Marketing at the University of Akron has developed twelve steps.[1] So why are there not eleven steps or ten steps? The reason is that each of the twelve steps to a successful direct marketing program is vital and cannot be overlooked.

Skipping over and around steps in developing a direct marketing strategy results in something like putting on your shoes before your socks. Each step provides information that refines and directs the strategy with the result that good direct marketing produces more results and less waste. The company, the competitor, and the product or service are key pieces of information to know that guide the final strategic initiative. Most importantly, this information enables a company to find and keep its best customers.

What are the twelve steps?

Customer Analysis

Profile your customer's needs, motivation, and buying profile. Ask yourself, "What do they buy, and why do they buy it?" For example, an Internet jewelry store knows that its customers do not tend to purchase expensive, authentic diamonds but at the same time would shy away from cubic zirconium. When a chance to purchase some moissanite comes along, they immediately see the value in making this offer to their consumers.

Environmental Analysis

Companies need to proactively anticipate not only the internal needs of their business, but also the next move of their competition that could potentially emerge. For example, rising gas prices shocked Americans and paved the way for a demand for hybrid vehicles that could be sold by dealers for higher-than-invoice prices. The environment provided a market for hybrid cars. Competitors were quick to respond with their own hybrid vehicles.

Figure 8.1 The direct marketing process.

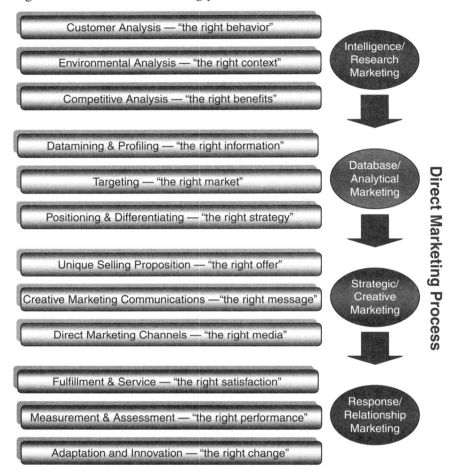

Competitive Analysis

Find out what your competitors are doing right and what they are doing wrong. This will be valuable help in developing your own message. For example, American Environmental Products obtained a patent for a new light designed to ward off the effects of seasonal affective disorder (SAD) in less than half the time of current products on the market. Knowing the competition allows this company to realize why their product will be desirable.

Data Mining and Profiling

Develop a database of prospects, then extract and analyze as much pertinent information as possible to get the best possible read on your audience. For example, customers who purchased the latest fat-busting, over-the-counter medication online received an e-mail about a newer product being touted as more effective. The computer system was designed to extract only those customers most likely to be interested.

Targeting

Further refine your database to figure out your best prospects. For example, offer customers who have shown themselves to be early adopters a great deal on the latest music device, knowing that they will likely be interested and they will show off their new gadget.

Positioning and Differentiating

Develop the offer, or central selling point, in a three-step process: identify the attributes of the offer and the characteristics that make it unique from your competitor's; delineate the benefits your customers will receive upon acceptance of the offer; and, finally, make claims that are the promised benefits for taking advantage of the offer. For example, bankless banking is a product of the Internet. Zopa (United Kingdom) and Prosper (United States) match those who want to borrow and those who want to lend in a process that bypasses banks altogether. They charge 1 percent of the amount of the loan. The claim is that lenders earn a higher rate than a savings account and borrowers pay less interest than a credit card.

Unique Selling Proposition

Shape the statement that conveys an implicit promise of a perceived value: it will make you more desirable, healthier, wealthier, wiser, and so on. For example, FedEx tells customers, "When it absolutely, positively has to get there overnight." UPS counters with, "What can Brown do for you today?" UPS uses the word "you" to personalize the message further.

Creative Marketing Communications

Determine how you will shape the message you have crafted. The message package involves each component of the media campaign, from the tone, to the typestyle, to the call to action. For example, Gatorade, one of the first sports drinks that promised to replenish lost electrolytes, has continued to be at the forefront of this niche in the beverage market thanks to their catchy television commercials, their colorful logo, and their lucrative endorsements at almost every college football game. Who has not seen the big Gatorade drum being overturned on the coach after a win? The company followed up with Propel and Endurance, other drinks for sports-minded individuals.

Direct Marketing Channels

Figure out how you will communicate your message. By mail? Newsletter? Phone call? Choose a direct marketing channel that will best get your pitch into the hearts and minds of your customers. For example, David Oreck's choice is television, where he demonstrates the company's eight-pound vacuum cleaner. Chadwick's, a women's clothing company, uses a catalog along with the Internet.

Fulfillment and Service

Let us say your prospect bites. How are you going to fill the order or request for a free sample or more information? Make sure your fulfillment and service operations run smoothly and conveniently for your buyers. For example, Country Curtains emphasizes customer service in every aspect of this catalog-Internet company headquartered in Massachusetts. Customer service employees are pictured in their catalog, right along with pictures of the company president. If something in your mail order does not look right, they call.

Measurement and Assessment

Track results so you know what you did right and wrong. Your campaign only worked if it cost-effectively bridged the barrier between you and your prospects. For example, Smucker's produces a line of snack products that are provided to airline passengers. They want to know if the products are well received and may possibly do an in-flight survey.

Adaptation and Innovation

Revise, refine, relaunch. If you are not totally happy with results, do not be afraid to tinker with the message, communications channel, or any other campaign element. For example, when Coca-Cola introduced New Coke, consumers rejected it overwhelmingly. The company relaunched its flagship product under a new name, Coke Classic, and advertised accordingly.

Robert A. MacKay, vice president of Internet sales and marketing for Step2 Corporation, summarized, "Direct marketing is a pivotal element of our marketing mix. It is bridging the gap between our best consumers and the hard-to-find products they desperately want. In the process, it is strengthening our relationships with them and sharpening our focus."[2]

Jay Lehman would agree with that. After many trips abroad, he saw the need to continue to produce various tools and implements when most companies no longer made them. The family's hardware store, Lehman's, is now the world's largest purveyor of historical products like those seen in *Pirates of the Caribbean*.

Is the strategy of direct marketing right for your company? Indeed, it is. Whether large or small, all companies can benefit from this direct marketing approach. Smaller companies with fewer resources can ill afford to throw money to the wind, so using marketing dollars wisely is essential. Larger companies also have a bottom line for marketing costs, and, in some cases, the marketing department will receive more funding when it has a proven strategy that works. Employing the direct marketing sequence is current, proactive, and understandable. Tim Searcy, CEO of the American Teleservices Association, stated, "Direct marketing is the fastest growing segment of the marketing and advertising space. Without a doubt, individuals with the education and skills to master the direct marketing process will have an enthusiastic reception in the marketplace."[3]

What happens when a company follows the twelve steps? The result is that the firm is bringing "good news" to their customers rather than aggravation and frustration. The result is that relationships are formed. The result is that the customer does not feel that his time is wasted. The result is that you are partnering with the customer, and then he or she sings your praises to everyone who shows an interest. And the Distribution Trap is avoided. Direct marketing is *the* way to bring about that kind of difference.

NOTES

1. The twelve-step process is elaborated upon in Andrew R. Thomas, Dale M. Lewison, William J. Hauser, and Linda M. Foley, eds., *Direct Marketing in Action: Cutting-Edge Strategies for Finding and Keeping the Best Customers* (Westport, CT: Praeger, 2006).

2. Ibid., p. 17.

3. Ibid., p. 19.

Chapter 9

GOING GLOBAL AND KEEPING
THE FAITH

The art of leadership is saying "no," not "yes." It is very easy
to say "yes."

—Tony Blair

A few years back, a U.S. firm that had a partnership in China manufacturing motorcycles went looking for new customers in Central
America. Previously, the U.S. firm had been relatively successful in
South America and Africa finding distributors for its line of basic
transportation motorcycles. With an engine design based on a
Honda model, the Chinese motorcycles were proven to be of acceptable quality and reliability. Most important, they were a lot cheaper:
about half the cost of the competing Japanese models.*

The entry point in Central America was Costa Rica, which,
along with Panama, was the most prosperous country in the
region. In addition to a growing economy and political stability,
other attractive conditions existed that might support strong
sales: especially a rising lower middle class that could now afford
motorcycles for basic transportation needs.

The American in charge of sales and distribution for the U.S.
firm was able to find two possible distributors in Costa Rica. Full
of pride because of earlier success in other markets, he believed

---

*This chapter is adapted from "It's the Distribution, Stupid," by Andrew R. Thomas
and Timothy J. Wilkinson, *Business Horizons*, 2005, vol. 48, pp. 125–134, by permission of publisher. Copyright © by Kelley School of Business, Indiana University. All
rights reserved.

himself invincible when it came to identifying who would be the best distributor in Costa Rica.

The first candidate was a young entrepreneur whose primary business was in the agriculture sector—especially importing farm implements and fertilizers. He had built a network of sales agents across Costa Rica. He believed the Chinese motorcycles— designed for and often used by farmers—would complement the current product offerings.

The second possibility, on the surface, however, seemed to be a wiser choice. The other firm was owned by one of the wealthiest men in all of Costa Rica and was the exclusive agent of Honda cars, Scania trucks, and Komatsu heavy equipment. A family business, the father previously had represented Honda motorcycles and the son was once again interested in lower-cost motorcycles. To the American, this option appeared to the best one for the distributorship of his firm's products.

Market research revealed to the U.S. firm that an annual sale of 250 motorcycles for each of the first three years was a reasonable expectation. This estimate was based on the total annual motorcycle imports for all of Costa Rica at around 2,700 units, with projected increases of 10 percent per year.

The American first sat down with the agricultural products distributor, who was very excited about the prospects of the Chinese motorcycles. Still, for the American, there was not a lot of satisfaction when the young man detailed his projections for only about 100 units annually. The young entrepreneur said it would take a long period of time for Costa Ricans to adapt to a Chinese model, but once it did happen, the potential would be enormous. Despite the enthusiasm, the American told his counterpart, "I will take your plan under advisement," and moved on. A short time later, the American was entering the sparkling facilities of the Honda/Scania/Komatsu distributor.

After an hour of discussions, the American offered the major player the exclusive distributorship for the Chinese motorcycles. The infrastructure of his company was quite impressive: the sales organization, service facilities, financial capabilities, and history of distribution with motorcycles were all outstanding. Moreover, the initial order was to be 1,000 units—four times what the American believed he could sell in the first year. The only remaining step was to prepare an agreement insuring the Costa Rican exclusive, sole rights for the first five years. Then, as soon as the agreement was formalized, a revolving Letter of Credit would be opened to ship the motorcycles in 125-unit increments over the first year.

Once the document was legalized, notarized, and signed, the first units were dispatched from China to Costa Rica. Everything was off to a great start. Nevertheless, when time came for the second shipment, things began to go bad. A document from the distributor to the confirming bank was required to reactivate the line of credit. It had not been sent. For several weeks, the American frantically tried to reach the Costa Rican distributor. He was always unavailable. When they did reach one of his many secretaries, the responses were always the same: "He's out of town . . . unavailable . . . in a meeting." As the next shipment of 125 bikes sat at the Port of Shanghai and the other 700 were in production, stress was getting a bit high for the American.

Without telling anyone, the American flew to San Jose to find out what was happening. He grabbed a taxi from the airport and headed straight to the distributor's office, where he was stiffly informed that the distributor "was unavailable for the rest of the week." Distraught, the American was further frustrated to see none of the motorcycles nor promotional material for his bikes anywhere at the facilities.

With no other option, the American hailed a taxi. As he was headed to his hotel, he was shocked to witness many small motorcycles cruising the streets of San Jose—something that he had not seen the last time he was there. Most of motorcycles were from his chief Taiwanese competitor.

After some time at the hotel bar to collect his thoughts, the American sucked it up and decided to call the first candidate—the one he turned down in favor of the rich guy. Absolutely uncertain what to expect, the American was blown away when the young man offered to meet for dinner. Clearly enjoying the moment, the Costa Rican showed some photographs of the American's motorcycles in their original crates, sitting in a bonded warehouse at the port of Limon. He then pulled out a recent newspaper article that stated that sales of Taiwanese-made motorcycles might exceed 500 units that year. As he read the article, the American discovered the last name of his exclusive distributor. It turns out his distributor's brother was bringing in the competition from Taiwan.

EXPORTING THE DYSFUNCTIONAL MODEL

It should not be surprising that many companies who are living the Distribution Trap at home do the same thing when they take their product overseas. This error is compounded by the fact that the most common option to enter into global markets is through distributors. Dishearteningly, even a cursory look at almost any international business college-level textbook has a most glaring omission: the issue of distribution is often left out. When it is dealt with, it is often as an issue of logistics. At best, the critical elements of selecting, bargaining with, and maintaining strong relationship with a global distributor are relegated to a few paragraphs.

Blue Sky Natural Beverage Co. demonstrates temptations from the Distribution Trap at the international level. The Santa Fe–based firm is a small $1.8 million natural juice drink producer. After spending a lot of time and money looking for a distributor in Japan, Blue Sky president Richard Becker found Cheerio Kansai, a soft-drink manufacturer located in Osaka. The distribution agreement that Blue Sky arranged with Kansai abrogated all of the control for the distribution of its product in Japan to the local agent.

As Megas often do at home, Cheerio ultimately redesigned Blue Sky's cans, ran ads that Blue Sky did not understand, paid 33 percent less than Blue Sky's Americans distributors did, and sold only two of the company's brands—ignoring everything else. Despite this maltreatment, Blue Sky justified the relationship under the guise that it could not afford its own office in Japan, had risked little, and, most important, had achieved an 8 percent increase in total sales as a result of Cheerio's first order.[1]

Fortunately, for Blue Sky, things did not end tragically. Nevertheless, what is revealed is the seductive nature of distribution-manufacturer relationships in the industrial world. In emerging markets, which are less economically and politically sophisticated, such an abrogation of control can lead to corporate disaster.

HOPE OUTSIDE THE UNITED STATES

The chance that American innovators will wrestle back control over the sales and distribution of their products at home is slim. The Megas in nearly every industry are fighting tooth and nail to maintain control. And while this may seem bleak—and it is bleak for those caught in the Distribution Trap—there is hope. The opportunity exists for innovators to regain control over the sales and distribution of their products—not at home, but in emerging markets overseas. In these places, manufacturers still have the opportunity to directly influence what happens to their products. Certainly, the Megas are trying to make their mark in Mexico, China, and Eastern Europe, but so far they have made few inroads. In fact, in many markets, the Megas have not done well at all. The window of opportunity is still open for manufacturers to shape and mold the way distribution is handled in these markets. The questions are and remain: Will they do it? And how can it be done the right way?

SEE IT FROM THE DISTRIBUTOR'S PERSPECTIVE

Academics who have looked at culture and international business always warn of the subconscious influence of self-reference-criteria (SRC) on corporate behavior and actions. SRC is the unconscious tendency to interpret a particular business situation through the lens of one's own cultural experience and value system.[2] Many examples of SRC are cited in the business literature. For example, an American who equates formality with agreement and is put off by the gregarious nature of his Argentine customer is experiencing the effects of SRC.

SRC can play an important factor in selecting international distributors. In the Costa Rican case, the ultimate candidate was the exclusive distributor of Honda cars, Scania trucks, and Komatsu heavy equipment. This distributor had stated that his company had also represented Honda motorcycles in the past. In reality, however, he was involved in a directly competing venture. This information was deliberately withheld from the American because the Costa Rican saw the arrival of the American not as an opportunity, but as a threat that needed to be eliminated.

Most emerging markets are characterized by high risk and uncertainty. In these places, opportunity is constrained by turbulent events that can destabilize a life's work almost overnight. Needless to say, control and predictability are of critical importance. In Costa Rica, rather than seeing the entrance of low-end motorcycles from China as an opportunity to grow market share, the distributor saw the entry of a new product as a present danger. For distributors in emerging markets, the environment is already full of uncertainty. Therefore, it is often best to lock foreign firms and other potential destabilizers out of the market. By entering into an agreement for exclusive distributorship in Costa

Rica, this individual was able to deftly eliminate what he perceived to be a problem.

SET MINIMAL AND IDEAL CRITERIA

To ensure the success of a distribution arrangement both parties
must bring something of value to the table.[3] The first question to be
answered for the manufacturer is, "What kind of distributor do you
want?" The answer to this question depends on circumstances and
on what goals need to be achieved. For overseas markets, distributor selection criteria should include consideration of distribution
outreach, functionality, appropriateness for products, cultural context, consumer-distributor interaction, and past performance.[4]

It is critical to set the qualities needed *before* undertaking the
screening and selection process. Once the criteria have been
established, it is vital to stick to your guns at all times. A new
environment, the uncertainty that accompanies exporting, and
the increased risk of operating in international markets, all con-
spire to convince new exporters to take the easy way out, to look
for a situation that feels good, in order to be comfortable with a
distributor. Do not fall for this temptation.

The criteria are left to the innovator. However, whatever they
end up being, you must be firm. Potential distributors should be
held accountable to a range of minimal and maximum characteristics. One recommendation is to consider whether a potential
distributor is involved with directly competitive products. In
emerging markets, the selection of a distributor like this almost
always leads to failure, especially for small and medium-sized
business.

Equally important, the innovator needs to look inwardly and
decide which things are going to be brought to the table, such as
exclusivity, patent and trademark protection, quality, favorable
pricing, training, new and improved products, and periodic visits.

FOCUS ON POTENTIAL COMPLEMENTORS

Like the domestic Distribution Trap, far too many American companies get burned when they choose an international distributor
who represent products similar to their own. The flawed logic of
the U.S. firm tends to go something like this:

We need to capture as much market share as we can. Instead of investing all of the resources necessary to mentor a distributor who doesn't really understand our products and services, it's easier to locate an existing distributor who has a history of handling products similar to ours. We'll educate them on what needs to be done in a couple of weeks. And then all they have to do is put our product into their pipeline. Fast, efficient, and to the point—just like we do it at home!

Nothing could be more wrong.

The best choice for an innovator's products in a given market is typically what we call a "complementor." This consists of a local company that represents and distributes goods that do nothing except enhance the image and perception of the innovator's products. In the Costa Rican example, the best choice was clearly the agricultural products distributor. The products that this distributor sold complemented the image of the motorcycle as a basic transportation vehicle for workers and farmers and could have opened a whole new market.

In Trinidad and Tobago, outdoor cookouts are a way of life. With around twenty-five national holidays per year and many weeks of vacation for the average worker, residents make full use of their abundant free time to host massive gatherings, where outdoor grilling is the centerpiece. Sensing a good opportunity, a U.S. producer of innovative natural gas and propane grills decided to explore the Trinidad and Tobago market.

On the surface, the best potential distributor seemed to be Choice Mart, a San Diego–based Mega that rivals Wal-Mart in Central America and the Caribbean. Choice Mart is the largest importer and distributor of grills in Trinidad and Tobago. And it is also the exclusive distributor for seven other brands of grills.

The U.S. company decided it did not want its innovations thrown onto shelves next to its direct competitors. Instead, it looked for a complementor in the market. In Trinidad and Tobago, most natural gas and propane is sold at gas stations. Three main companies controlled the service center market and the U.S. company decided that such complementors would make for an ideal distributor. In just a few short months, the U.S. innovator was number two in the marketplace.

Loctite, a Connecticut-based company that specializes in adhesives, initially partnered with distributors who were well versed with the local market because these distributors carried competitors products. After experiencing the negative consequences of having the market controlled by the distributor, Loctite began to seek out complementors—firms that they called "company fit" rather than "market fit." According to one executive, "The closeness of the market fit can be a liability as well as an asset, because the distributors represent the market's status quo, and we are selling a replacement technology and attempting to change the market."[5] In contrast, company-fit partners, while unable to generate quick, short-term sales, are distributors willing to invest in the relationship in terms of time and willing to be trained in the product.

EXPLICITLY SPELL OUT RESPONSIBILITIES

As with children, responsibilities need to be defined and explained so that both parties have clear expectations. If not viewed correctly, a well-written distribution contract will provide false hope to a manufacturer that it really is in control. This is natural given the detail and complexity of most agreements as well as the time, energy, and cost required to produce them. However, too often companies do not recognize the limitations of these legal instruments.

International distributor agreements falsely create the impression that the document itself has generated business. If an innovator wants to successfully sell and distribute its products in a new market, it will need more than merely a document prepared by and agreed to by lawyers. Distribution can only be successful if both parties are highly motivated. The key to selling and distributing products in a global market is not just a legal document, but the development of mutually beneficial relationships and a strong, effective business strategy.

Still, a well-crafted distributor agreement can and does provide a degree of security against badly intentioned individuals who are seeking to hurt the manufacturer and impede market entry. John Deere, like so many major U.S. manufacturers attempting to enter the Middle East years ago, was being wooed into signing a blanket agreement that allowed a local distributor to operate with impunity. Large initial purchase orders were dangled in front of the company as a temptation to throw caution to the wind. John Deere, however, saw through the scheme and presented a thirty-page distribution agreement that was so comprehensive and thorough, it scared off the potential "distributor." In this case, the agreement served as an instrument to better qualify and assess the credibility of a potential distributor.

CONSTRUCT THE RELATIONSHIP

An international distributor agreement should be viewed as the starting point in an ongoing and evolving relationship. Unlike the United States and Western Europe, where a robust legal system ensures the relative integrity of business transactions, the legal infrastructure within emerging markets is usually unstable and unpredictable. In India and China, for example, contracts are often written with clever phrases, small print, and all manner of trickery. Such contractual aggression is made possible by poorly developed legal and regulatory regimes and court proceedings that require a great deal of time and money. Control or governance of foreign distributors is most effective when it is the result of relational norms developed and implemented by the manufacturer.

U.S. manufacturers tend to complain that distributors do not know how to grow the market, and that they are only interested in what is accessible, and that they under-invest in the relationship. Distributors, in other words, are often viewed as lacking ambition and as not caring about the relationship. Conversely, U.S. companies tend to view international distributors as only a temporary expediency that can be jettisoned after adequate market traction positions them to open up their own subsidiaries. However, owning subsidiaries is an expensive and time-intensive venture. Rather than viewing distributors as merely a quick way to enter a market, manufacturers should work carefully with their distributors to help them develop the business for the long term. David Arnold, who studied the relationships of 250 manufacturers and distributors, characterized success as follows:

> They acted as if they were business partners with the multinationals. They shared market information with the corporations; they initiated projects with distributors in neighboring countries; and they suggested initiatives in their own or nearby markets. These managers risked investing in areas such as training, information systems, and advertising and promotion in order to grow the multinationals' business.[6]

CONSTANTLY SCRUTINIZE THE RELATIONSHIP

A number of standards exist that manufacturers can use to scruti-
nize the performance of a distributor. These standards include sales
performance, inventory management, selling capabilities, attitudes,
competition facing distributors, and general growth potential.

Again, it may seem foreign to a U.S. company, but it is quite
possible to have control over the sales and distribution of products in an emerging market. This is accomplished by exercising
due diligence and staying on top of their distributor's performance in a timely fashion.

MANAGE COMMUNICATION

Part of the due diligence of U.S. firms must also include a communication plan that ensures the quality and quantity of interaction
between parties. A successful communication strategy is twofold.
The first part of the strategy should deal with operational components such as purchase orders, delivery, inventory, payments, and
pricing. The second part should influence the distributor's behavior.
Personal selling, advertising, sales promotions, and so on, are used
to instill the corporate vision of the innovator into their distributor.

Challenges should be expected between partners when it
comes to effective communication. Physical separation, differen-
ces in size, organization type, operating procedures, and native
languages will enter in at one time or another. These challenges
are further compounded because most emerging market distributors forge their business relationships on a foundation of inherent
distrust of even their closest associates.

Another issue that is often overlooked is that of confidentiality
in communications. Stories abound where executives traveling
overseas have been offered the opportunity to purchase faxes or
e-mails from or to their competitors by enterprising hotel clerks.
In many markets, it is not uncommon for meeting rooms, mobile
phones, cars, and hotel suites to be bugged by local distributors.

INCENTIVIZE THE RELATIONSHIP

In addition to monitoring, exporters can influence the behavior
of distributors by offering appropriate incentives. Rather than

providing standard operating procedures to control the behavior of the distributor, a laissez-faire approach focuses on outcomes by offering incentives and imposing penalties. The firm is compensated when and if sales occur, and it is penalized if sales do not occur.

PC Globe, a Tempe, Arizona–based software company, initially offered distributors exclusivity without establishing any standards of performance. Not surprisingly, their overseas sales were disappointing. Eventually, the firm changed its approach. In exchange for exclusivity, a distributor must now order and prepay 20 percent of what they think they can sell in their first year. The exclusivity is guaranteed as long as they continue to order the same amount each quarter. According to company executives, these distributors "don't get exclusivity as much as the opportunity for exclusivity."[7]

CONCLUSION

Although its critical importance cannot be overstated, distribution is generally the most globally differentiated and least understood of all marketing mix components. It is also the component most likely to hinder success in foreign markets, especially for small and mid-size companies. Proper distribution planning can ensure that the best available channels and distribution methods are in place to efficiently and economically move products and services to customers.

The process for establishing successful sales and distribution strategies in high-growth emerging markets is formidable. We recommend that managers analyze the situation from the perspective of the distributor, set clear criteria for distributor selection, search out and work with firms marketing complementary products, make sure that expectations are explicit and clear, build a long-term relationship with the distributor, and monitor the relationship and provide appropriate incentives to keep the relationship on track. Through the application of these strategies, manufacturers will be better able to maximize opportunities found in global markets.

In the case of the motorcycle manufacturer who was badly burned in Costa Rica, the lessons from that experience slowly found their way into the corporate culture of the organization. Although many mistakes persisted in recruiting and selecting foreign distributors, the American firm slowly began to realize the critical importance of breaking out of the dysfunctional domestic distribution model and establishing something new and much more dynamic.

Immediately after the Costa Rica debacle, mental checklists and queries among the staff preceded most discussions about new business. As the organization began to adjust its culture to the realities of global distribution, processes for distribution selection were formalized. Ultimately, minimally acceptable criteria were established. Three years later, the achieved distributor retention rate was well over 80 percent, and, not surprisingly, sales and revenues were up more than 60 percent. The result was a series of mutually beneficial relationships in which the manufacturer was firmly in control of the sales and distribution of its products.

NOTES

1. John B. Cullen, *Multinational Management: A Strategic Approach* (Cincinnati, OH: South-Western College Publishing, 1999), p. 156.

2. James S. Lee, "Cultural Analysis in Overseas Operations," *Harvard Business Review*, March–April 1966, pp. 106–114.

3. Steven E. Harbour, "Five Rules of Distribution Management," *Business Horizons* 40, no. 3 (1997): 53–59.

4. A. Coskun Samli, *Entering and Succeeding in Emerging Countries.* (Mason, OH: South-Western Educational and Professional Publishing, 2004), p. 48.

5. David Arnold, "Seven Rules of International Distribution," *Harvard Business Review*, November–December 2000, p. 135.

6. Arnold, "Seven Rules of International Distribution," p. 132.

7. Inc.com, "Exclusivity vs. Temporary Monopoly," available at http://pf.inc.com/articles/1995/01/11160.html (accessed January 2009).

Chapter 10

DISTRIBUTION: THE KEY TO THE SUSTAINABLE ENTERPRISE

The ability to learn faster than your competitors may be the only sustainable competitive advantage.

—Arie de Geus

Churning out 6 percent of global supply, the Faun Textile mill in southern China is the largest producer of knit cotton in the world. Located on a 230-acre campus, it has spent the last two decades producing the material that goes into inexpensive jeans, sneakers, and T-shirts, for dozens of American retailers, including Wal-Mart, Target Corporation, Eddie Bauer, Nike, and Lands' End. The factory is owned by Fountain Set Holdings Ltd., a Hong Kong–based firm that places most of its effort into manufacturing the soft stretch cotton that goes into T-shirts and sweatshirts. The Megas typically work with Fountain Set to determine colors and seasonal fabric styles, although they usually buy the company's products through a third party that takes the material and turns it into clothing.

In the summer of 2006, villagers in Dongguan, the city where the Faun Textile mill is located, noticed that the Mao Zhou River running through their city had turned blood red. An investigation by local officials revealed that a pipe buried beneath the factory floor was dumping about 22,000 tons of contaminated water into the river each day. While this was noteworthy in Dongguan, it was of little interest downriver where runoff from hundreds of manufacturing plants have created a river of thick, oily sludge, covered with plastic bags, electrical wires, shoes, and other items. Li Changlin, a small businessman who works downstream from the Faun Textile mill, said, "We used to eat fish and crayfish out of this river . . . we swam in it. There were green plants on the banks and the water was clear. After 1989, the factories came and the water turned black."[1] Unfortunately, the Faun Textile mill incident and the polluted Mao Zhou River are not isolated instances in China. Rather, the largest country in the world is also one of the most polluted, and this pollution is largely caused by the Distribution Trap. Meanwhile, the textile plants in the United States are mostly out of business.

The environmental degradation taking place in China and other emerging countries is due to phenomenal economic development taking place at a breakneck pace. While many factors contribute to high levels of pollution in these nations, the role that the Megas play in distributing products to Americans is front and center. This role is evident when looking at how product quality and product price interact with the distribution channel that brings the desired merchandise to the U.S. market.

GENERIC PRODUCT STRATEGY

Political, social, historical, and economic factors in the United States, Europe, and Japan have created identifiable, "generic" product strategies that are used by companies in their respective regions of the world to create sustainable competitive advantage. The strategies used are based on trade-offs between price and quality.[2]

Nations encompass dissimilar sources of competitive advantages that either shape the firms that exist within their boundaries or that can be tapped into by those firms. These include the cost of raw materials, competitive environment, business climate, and circumstances involving the needs and wants of domestic consumers. These forces shape attitudes about both price and quality, and, as a result, catalyze the trade-offs people are willing to make as they purchase goods.

UNITED STATES

Firms in the United States pursue an "economy" product strategy that emphasizes lower quality at a lower price. In other words, Americans like cheap stuff and they are not overly concerned about durability or reliability. If an item wears out or breaks down, a cheap replacement can always be purchased. People over the age of fifty can attest that this has not always been the case, but, as anyone who has purchased a DVD player lately knows, this is the way products now are manufactured. The economy strategy is based on a number of factors. First, U.S. companies are under unyielding pressure to maximize short-run returns on investment. This short-term orientation has led to underinvestment in long-term process development and underinvestment in manufacturing systems that are needed to produce higher-quality products. The outsourcing of American manufacturing to China has surely reinforced the tendency to underinvest.

American managers are rewarded when they effectively use short-term marketing tactics such as price cutting and advertising. Human resource practices, which encourage high employee turnover, have been directly correlated with lower quality. Because higher-quality strategies involve a longer time frame, managers who are rewarded according to short-term performance are likely to pursue lower-quality strategies.

The U.S. competitive environment also facilitates the "economy" strategy of American firms. U.S. investors are interested in short-term profit maximization. In Japan, people are likely to buy and hold; in the United States, putting money into the stock market is more akin to gambling, as demonstrated by the complex leveraging undertaken by investment banks that so contributed to the 2008 economic meltdown. Compared with European and Japanese companies, American firms place great emphasis on the need for a high return on investment. This has reinforced the need for outsourcing to lower costs, and it has led to the neglect of process development in favor of product development, branding, and marketing. These short-term strategies, in turn, lead to lower-quality products and price-based competition.

American consumers are far more price sensitive than are their Japanese or European counterparts. While the latter might fret about product quality, Americans are fixated on price. Harvard's Michael Porter says this may be because the United States was the first "mass production and consumption" society. Consumers became used to ever-decreasing prices and, over time, developed a taste for disposable products. Porter writes:

> No longer is America the nation that always foreshadows the world market. No longer is America so consistently the home of the

world's most sophisticated buyers. The American consumer and the American industrial buyer, then, no long represent as great a strength as they once did. The result is an inability of American firms to keep pace in innovation and with the differentiation strategies of foreign rivals. The upgrading of American industries then falters. American consumers are often no longer the most affluent. They are certainly not the most demanding. They tolerate products and services that no Japanese or German would.[3]

Baby boomers will remember the television repairman. This individual who would come to your house to fix your television has long since gone the way of the milk man and the ice wagon. Because American consumers want "economy" products, U.S. firms are obliged to respond. The goods that result are not expected to be of particularly high quality or to last a long time. This is America's "throw-away society" in action, and it contributes to the lower-price/lower-quality orientation of U.S. companies.

EUROPEAN UNION

Firms in the countries of the European Union—here we are referring primarily to the fifteen nations of the European Union prior to the addition of Eastern European countries after 2004—pursue a premium generic product strategy. The products they sell tend to be of a comparatively higher quality and cost than what you would find in the United States or Japan. Any American tourist traveling through Europe is both impressed by the quality of European products and services as well as the high price of *everything*. "How do these people afford to live" is the common question of the American traveler. In a recent trip to Vienna, a friend was alarmed when she walked by the Austrian version of the dollar store, "The 18 Euro Store."

The fact is, European society is set up in such a way that the Europeans absolutely must be able to command high prices for their products. They cannot do otherwise because the political economy of the European Union demands that high-quality, high-priced items be produced and purchased to support the vast welfare state that developed during the postwar era.

After World War II, the countries of Western Europe pursued what came to be known as "industrial policy." This consisted of a mixed economy in which some industrial sectors were in private hands, and other sectors, particularly heavy industry, were owned by governments. Examples include auto manufacturer British Leyland, the National Freight Corporation, British Airways, British Petroleum, British Telecom, Jaguar, and British Airways. The coal mines were owned and operated by the government as were the railroads. Similar forms of government ownership existed across Europe. While privatization has occurred, particularly in the United Kingdom, industrial policy is still prevalent in much of Europe. The economies are characterized by heavy taxation of business to support the "welfare state," including national health care and retirement pensions. Obviously, this increases the cost of doing business. A less direct cost involves extensive regulations intended to protect employee rights in the workplace. This drives up costs indirectly by forcing European businesses to operate inefficiently. For example, firing employees in Belgium and Portugal is extremely difficult and costly; Sweden provides 480 days of paid parental leave, for both the mother and the father, in connection with childbirth; and France provides unemployment benefits that are about three times as generous as those found in the United States and Britain. European companies also emphasize long-term employment and worker participation, which contribute to product quality through better employee knowledge and motivation.

All of this adds up. With high taxes and labor costs, European firms eschew low-cost strategies in favor of producing higher value-added products. In fact, they must produce high-quality products because they need to be able to charge a premium price. Harvard's Michael Porter says, "German firms almost inevitably [compete] on the basis of differentiation, not cost. They upgrade products continuously and almost invariably gravitate to the high-performance product segments, as in cutlery, cars, and printing presses."[4]

European consumers also contribute to the high-quality focus of European manufacturers. Retailers tend to be highly specialized and are able to provide information to Europe's picky and sophisticated customers. Quality is more important to Europeans than it is to Americans. "We would rather have two or three nice suits," a Belgian business woman told us, "than a closet full of low-quality clothes." Lance Eliot Brouthers and his co-authors, who came up with the idea of generic product stereotypes state, "This combination of high quality sensitivity coupled with low price sensitivity helps to create a market ideally suited for premium-product strategies."[5]

Distribution in the European Union

Historically, the national, cultural, and historical context of Europe has created markets that are highly fragmented and heterogeneous. This market structure has in turn resulted in small to midsize firms capable of adapting to, and prospering in, a highly segmented market environment. With few exceptions, the largest European companies have not operated as pan-European giants but as national companies, avoiding the many encumbrances of functioning across borders where market conditions are so dissimilar.

Europe's highly fragmented markets have resulted in firms that pursue niche strategies. These strategies emphasize craftsmanship, specialization, and networks of relationships. Because companies cannot fully exploit the economies of scale and scope inherent in large homogenous markets, they are unable to compete on the basis of low cost or low price.

In their classic article, "Globalization Frustrated: The Case of White Goods," Charles Baden-Fuller and John Stopford summarized distribution in Europe:

> The continental scope of Sears Roebuck is widely credited as having had an important influence in unifying the previously disparate regional markets within the U.S.A. (Hunt, 1972). No equivalent distributor has yet emerged within Europe, where retailing is heavily concentrated within national borders. . . . Powerful national retailers can favor nationally focused producers, as does Marks and Spencer in British textiles and Electricity Boards in both white and brown goods. . . . Moreover, national associations such as local chambers of commerce in France and Germany, can also distort demand and limit the international extent of the strategic market, and thus the profitability of a global strategy.[6]

A major purpose of the European Union is to create extensive homogeneous markets. One expert stated, "The goal is to develop large European companies able to take advantage of economies of scale so that these firms are better equipped to compete with their American counterparts."[7] The implementation of a common currency in many of the EU countries, coupled with coordinated economic policies, has encouraged the defragmentation of markets in Europe. However, despite progress, cultural, political, economic, and social forces persist. The continent has a long way to go before it can be considered the United States of Europe.

JAPAN

In contrast to both the United States and the European Union, the Japanese product strategy tends to emphasize comparatively higher quality at relatively lower prices. During the postwar period, the Japanese financial sector operated under the supervision and direction of government bureaucracy. "Window guidance" was the term used to describe the Japanese government's encouragement of banks to aggressively lend to preselected firms. Japan's industrial policy is directed by the Ministry of Economy, Trade and Industry (METI) formerly abbreviated as MITI. METI has many tools at its disposal to carry out the country's goal of economic nationalism. Its structure is fascinating:

> It maintains an exhaustive information-gathering apparatus and performs numerous "think tank" functions, establishing "long-term visions" of various industrial structures of the future. It is organized with vertical bureaus, demarcated by industry, and capable of implementing industrial policy at the microeconomic level. It indirectly influences the allocation of capital at crucial pressure points throughout the economy, resulting in differential growth rates yielding altered structures in concert with strategic goals. Means are found to reward cooperative companies and punish the uncooperative. While keeping in mind the need to adjust to changing market conditions, MITI shapes and alters market forces and accepts the market's judgments of the success or failure of such initiatives. Finally, MITI's visions are not born in bureaucratic isolation, but rather reflect endless discussions with industrialists, financial leaders, journalists, academics, and of course politicians.[8]

The result of this vision was heavy capital investment in specific industries such as automobiles and consumer electronics. These industries do not exhibit the typical positive association between price and quality because economies of scale coupled with increased experience means that quality improves even as prices drop. Unlike the European Union, the Japanese do not have to charge higher prices for premium products to finance a comprehensive welfare state. As an export-led economy, they charge high prices at home to subsidize lower prices abroad.

The production of high-quality products has been at the heart of Japanese corporate culture for decades. The Japanese have been early adopters of quality initiatives, from Total Quality

Management, to Quality Circles, to the more recent adoption of Six Sigma. Process innovations are used to consistently cut costs and improve product quality. It all goes back to a presentation made by Dr. W. Edwards Deming, in 1950, to a prestigious business association. He demonstrated how statistical methods could be used to improve consistency and quality in industrial production. Deming's ideas became popular, and today the most prestigious quality award in Japan is the "Deming Prize."

Porter argues that countries with fierce internal competition are more likely to have innovative companies. Competition encourages firms to make incremental improvements in production processes and product development. Unlike Europe, where governments have subsidized specific companies that are viewed as "national champions," the Japanese have encouraged domestic competition. This has created a sophisticated supplier base in Japan in which industrial buyers have high expectations and suppliers are continuously pushed toward innovation. An institutional commitment to quality pervades the entire manufacturing sector of the Japanese economy.

Japan is the home of extremely sophisticated consumers. Porter says that they are "notoriously picky." This contributes to the quality emphasis of Japanese firms. Porter states the following:

> Pressure from demanding and sophisticated buyers is widespread in Japanese consumer industries. Japanese consumers will reject a product because of a small surface defect, one reason for the attention of Japanese companies to "fits and finishes." Customers demand high quality and superior service. Japan has a visual culture, in which the presentation, and the packaging, are as important as the product. Japanese consumers are also fickle in comparison to those in most other nations. They will readily switch brands if a quality difference is noticeable. The sophistication of Japanese buyers is reinforced by an extreme abundance of product information.[9]

Why do the Japanese not pursue a premium strategy given their ability to create high-quality products? Certainly, the Japanese must be leaving money on the table considering their engineering is widely considered to be every bit as good as the Europeans. The reason for the lower margins is what marketing strategist Kenichi Ohmae called "the Japanese instinct to build share at any cost."[10] Japan has an export-oriented economy that has achieved its success by seizing industrial sectors previously dominated by American companies. It has accomplished this by competing on the basis of price while tenaciously implementing product and process improvements. It is no accident that Toyota is now the world's largest automaker, that seven of the top twenty semiconductor companies are Japanese, or that Japan is the dominant producer of machine tools and consumer electronics.

Distribution in Japan

Japanese marketing channels are multilayered and fragmented. They have been characterized as "complex, confusing, inefficient, and archaic."[11] Japan is a country of small mom-and-pop retail stores. Small-scale stores historically have been the rule. Manufacturers in the cosmetics, appliance, and automobile sectors have controlled distribution by establishing their own sales companies, using exclusive retailers, and organizing specific sales channels.

The integration of distribution into corporate groupings, called *keiretsu*, is a traditional strategy that manufacturers have used to gain preferential treatment for their products while excluding those of competitors. For example, automobile manufacturers use *keiretsu* to function as exclusive dealer networks that sell only a limited number of makes.[12] Similarly, in Japan, a "designated agent" system limits the number of wholesalers that handle processed foods and everyday goods.[13]

There is a huge number of retailers in Japan. Although this number has been decreasing since 1985, the tradition of mom-and-pop stores persists. In 2004, the country had 1,238,049 retail establishments. In that year, Japan's population peaked at 127,790,000—that equates to one store for about every 100 people.[14] By way of contrast, the United States had 1,119,849 retail establishments in 2004, about one store for every 257 people.[15] This reflects both the relative size of retail stores in the United States compared with Japan, as well as the sheer number of retail outlets.

Japan's byzantine system of distribution has been labeled a "nontariff trade barrier" by critics in the United States who have charged that its markets have remained relatively closed even after the elimination of formal trade barriers. The inability of the Megas to crack the Japanese market illustrates how Japan's use of nontariff barriers is used to keep competitors out of the country. One weapon in the nontariff barrier arsenal was known as the "Large-Scale Retail Law." Passed in 1974, this law was intended to protect small to medium-size stores by heavily regulating establishments larger than 500 square meters. The law was amended a number of times, with each amendment further constricting the freedom of retailers with large-scale ambitions. One of the requirements was that the developer of the large retail store had to obtain the consent of local shopkeepers before a building permit would be granted. Toys"R"Us, for example, encountered enormous difficulties when it attempted to enter Japan in the 1980s. After years of legal and bureaucratic obstruction, a store was opened on the outskirts of Tokyo in 1991. The Large-Scale Retail Law "turned Japan into one of the few countries in the Pacific region that heavily regulat[ed] domestic distribution."[16]

In the 1980s, the United States leaned heavily on the Japanese government, insisting that the law be repealed and that Japan open up to foreign business. This took place early in the Clinton administration. Even as Japan phased out the Large-Scale Retail Law, however, it passed something called "The Law Concerning Measures by Large-Scale Retail Stores for the Preservation of the Living Environment." Instead of relying on objections from local shop owners, this law empowered local governments to pass ordinances to ensure that store plans would meet national environmental protection standards.

IMPACT ON THE ENVIRONMENT

Accessing the mass market through the Megas means that American companies are forced to outsource manufacturing to China, where a lack of environmental protection leads to phenomenal amounts of air and water pollution. In return, China exports products to the United States that are sold through the Megas and, because of low quality, quickly end up in America's 3,091 landfills.

Figure 10.1 shows the growth of municipal waste in relation to U.S. retail trade from 1960 to 2006.[17] During this period, municipal solid waste grew from 88.1 million tons to 251.3 million tons, an almost threefold increase, while solid waste per capita nearly doubled. During the same period, the contribution of retail trade to gross domestic product quadrupled. According to the

Figure 10.1 Municipal solid waste generation and retail trade.

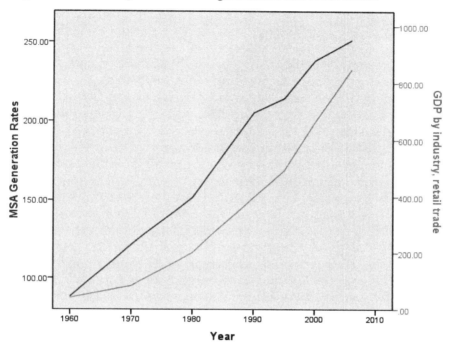

Environmental Protection Agency (EPA), 55 to 65 percent of municipal waste is classified as "residential waste." In other words, it is the product of the buying habits of individuals and families. The largest component of municipal waste is organic material, followed by paper and paperboard products. Figure 10.2 gives a detail of waste generation according to product category for 2007. Note that containers and packaging represent the largest category, followed by nondurable goods (things like books, newspapers, towels, and trash bags). Perhaps the most obvious symbol of the increase in household waste that has occurred since World War II is the nonrefillable beverage container. Beer and soft drink cans made up less than 5,000 tons or 0.05 percent of municipal waste in 1960. In 1970, this number stood at 100,000 tons of waste; by 2007, it was 1,420,000 tons.

The phenomenal increase in the generation of residential solid waste has occurred in tandem with the low-price, low-quality strategy of the American Mega distributors. An examination of

Figure 10.2 Total municipal waste in 2007 by product category (254 million tons, before recycling).

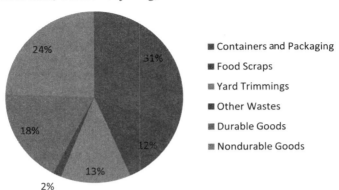

- Containers and Packaging
- Food Scraps
- Yard Trimmings
- Other Wastes
- Durable Goods
- Nondurable Goods

municipal waste per capita is instructive. In 1960, a single American produced, on average, 2.68 pounds of waste each day. By 1990, this had increased to 4.5 pounds per day with only incremental increases since then. This roughly parallels the rise of the Megas. Over the last twenty-five years, as consumer prices have dropped and as consumption has increased, people have purchased more and more cheap stuff that quickly wears out and is then discarded.

Solid waste presents a huge problem for future generations of Americans. While the number of landfills has declined dramatically during past twenty years (from 7,924 in 1988 to 1, 754 in 2007), average landfill size has increased, and raw tonnage has increased from 205.2 million tons in 1990 to 254.1 million tons in 2007. Of the municipal waste generated in the United States, around 65 percent ends up in a landfill, with the rest either incinerated or recycled.[18]

Despite recycling and composting efforts, many discarded products are not recovered through these programs. Elizabeth Royte tracked the trajectory of her family's garbage in her book *Garbage Land: On the Secret Trail of Trash*.[19] Among her discoveries was that the landfill decomposition process is laden with uncertainties. She stated, "depending on its burial context, a Granny Smith apple can biodegrade completely in two weeks or last several thousand years."[20] Of even greater concern is plastic. It turns out that plastic is difficult to recycle. She explained,

"Streams of mixed plastic can be turned into only one other product (plastic wood, garden pavers, or toothbrush handles, for example). When their useful life is over, these products cannot be 'recycled' again. They have to be burned or buried. Either way they add toxins to the environment."[21] According to the EPA, only 11.7 percent of all plastics were recovered for recycling in 2007. The numbers look a bit better for plastic containers, for which the recovery rate was 28 percent for plastic milk and water bottles and 36.6 percent for plastic soft drink bottles. The rest of it ends up in the landfill.

Figure 10.3 lists municipal waste generation by country. In the United States, each person generates about 1,584 pounds of municipal waste every year. This is 286 pounds more than the nearest EU-15 country, Luxembourg, which generates 1,298 pounds per person. Citizens in Britain generate fully 500 pounds less than Americans and the people of Sweden produce only half of that of Americans. The Europeans, with their higher-quality, higher-priced goods, simply have less to throw away and are more likely to hold onto what they have than their American counterparts.

Interestingly, Japan is near the bottom of the pack, generating about 880 pounds of municipal waste per person. This conforms to the generic product/price strategy pursued in the United States, the European Union, and Japan and conforms to the

Figure 10.3 Municipal waste generation in 2000 by country.
Sources: Adapted from Organisation for Economic Co-operation and Development (OECD) Environmental Data Compendium, 2002, via NationMaster.

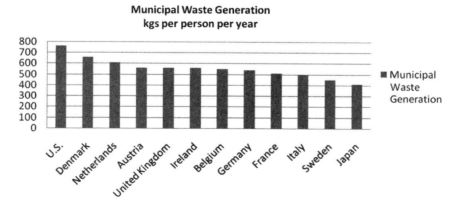

distribution pattern of the firms in each country. Europeans, with their purchases of comparatively higher-quality/higher-priced products produced and distributed through fragmented markets, generate less waste than their American counterparts. Similarly, the Japanese, with their focus on relatively higher-quality products sold through multilevel distribution channels, produce almost half the waste. Other factors besides generic product strategy and the prevalent pattern of distribution no doubt come into play. At the same time, it is striking to note that the country with the dominant Megas is the one with the highest waste per person.

ENVIRONMENT DAMAGE IN THE MEGA'S SUPPLY CHAIN

Perhaps the biggest environmental damage takes place through the supply chains that feed products into the Megas. In 1990, Chile sold 28,810 tons of salmon. In 2007, it produced 664,661 tons. The impetus behind the increase was Wal-Mart and Costco, which buy at least half the salmon that is imported into the United States from Chile. What used to be a specialty food shipped to the lower forty-eight states from Alaska was made widely available by the Megas when Wal-Mart went into the grocery business and began to sell salmon for less than $5 a pound. In Chile, salmon is farm raised along the country's mountainous coastline. With more than sixty companies operating there, it is the second-largest exporter of the product.

Circumstances surrounding farm-raised salmon have been likened to hog farming. Gerry Leape, the vice president of a Washington-based environmental group stated:

> These fish are the hogs of the sea. They live in the same sort of conditions [as hogs], it's just in water. They pack them really closely together, they use a lot of prophylactic antibiotics, not to treat disease, but to prevent it. There's lots of concentrated fish waste, it creates dead zones in the ocean around the pens.[22]

The pens used for the salmon are ninety-eight feet by ninety-eight feet and typically contain 80,000 fish in the early stages of the process. These conditions are favorable to a variety of diseases, including Ricketsia (spotted fever) and infectious salmon anemia (I.S.A.). Dr. Felipe C. Cabello, a professor of microbiology and immunology at New York Medical College, estimates that Chilean producers use 70 to 300 times more antibiotics in their salmon production than do producers in Norway. Heavy use of antibiotics is required to counteract the disease-ridden environment in which the salmon are raised. In 2008, the government of Chile took steps to improve sanitary conditions and reduce the use of antibiotics after a virus killed millions of the penned salmon. These steps have been taken because conditions became so deplorable that access to the U.S. market was threatened.

China is the poster child of environmental degradation. With economic growth averaging 9.9 percent a year since 1978, the Chinese have largely ignored environmental concerns in their quest for development. The outsourcing compulsion (described in Chapter 5) has forced firms to lower costs by offshoring production, much of it to China. However, the benefits of incoming foreign direct investment (FDI) have come at a high cost. China's coal-and-cement towns, covered with black soot and gray cement dust, are reminiscent of 19th-century London. James Fallows, writing in *The Atlantic Monthly*, stated, "Driving through the foothills of the Tibetan plateau in western Sichuan province last year, my wife and I could tell from miles away when we were nearing a cement plant from the grayish pall in the air and the thickening layers of dust on the trees and road."[23]

Pollution in China is of legendary proportions. In rural areas, drinking water standards are frequently ignored for both piped and nonpiped water, leaving about 500 million people without access to safe drinking water. The result is chemical and inorganic land-based contamination that washes into the water supply leading to high death rates resulting from stomach, liver, and bladder cancer.

The country's industrial cities are so full of air pollution that their occupants rarely see the sun. This is the case even though sulfur dioxide (SO_2) and particulate levels have been in decline since the 1980s. SO_2 is a by-product of the combustion of coal and petroleum. In the United States, the percentage of tons of SO_2 released into the atmosphere has steadily declined since 1970. In China, SO_2 levels have increased despite reduction targets set by the government. This is because China is second only to the United States as a consumer of energy, and its energy comes from a dirty source—coal burned in industrial boilers or thermal power plants. In addition to SO_2, the heavy reliance on coal has polluted the air with suspended particulates, which are fine particles of liquid or solids that

float in the air. These particulates—and China has lots of them float-
ing around—are associated with respiratory problems and heart
disease. Fifty percent of Chinese cities do not meet air-quality standards set by the government.

Lead poison and other toxins have killed or sickened scores
of children in China. The coastline no longer supports marine
life because it is crowded with algal red tides. Of the twenty
most polluted cities in the world, sixteen are in China.[24] In
2007, Chinese officials censored the report, "Cost of Pollution in
China," produced jointly by the World Bank and several minis-
tries of the Chinese government. Censored sections stated that
750,000 people die prematurely each year from pollution-related
diseases. Of these deaths, 300,000 resulted from the inhalation
of fumes from coal-burning stoves and about 60,000 were attributed to cancers and diarrhea caused by water pollution in rural
areas.

The low-price strategy of the Megas has driven their suppliers
to developing countries where inadequate environmental laws
and enforcement damages the environment and the health of the
people living there. American manufacturers, forced overseas by
the Megas, have engaged in various forms of FDI, including
wholly owned subsidiaries, joint ventures, and contract manufacturing. Each of these takes place in developing countries where
environmental laws are lax or not enforced. These countries may
be viewed favorably by multinationals because they constitute
"pollution havens" where the cost of pollution is absorbed by the
people living in those countries, not by the multinational corporations or their customers. Often, companies that serve the Megas
enter these countries naively through contract manufacturing.
The consulting firm A. T. Kearney estimates that 23 percent of
FDI consists of "contractual joint ventures."[25] The environmental
damage that occurs is the result of domestic companies that simply manufacture products according the specification of their
American corporate customers.

The offshoring of production, driven by the Megas, is not sustainable. China and other emerging economies have traded
extremely high economic growth for polluted air, water, and
land. No country can pursue such a strategy indefinitely. In the
coming decades, as emerging markets grow up, environmental
concerns will outweigh the appetite for growth, and the unrea-
sonably low prices that Americans have come to expect as they
make purchases from the Megas will end.

NOTES

1. Jane Spencer, "Ravaged Rivers: China Pays Steep Price as Textile Exports Boom," *Wall Street Journal*, August 22, 2007.

2. The discussion of generic product strategy is based on the following paper: Lance Eliot Brouthers, Steve Werner, and Erika Matulich, "The Influence of Triad Nations' Environments on Price-Quality Product Strategies and MNC Performance," *Journal of International Business Studies* 31, no. 1 (2000).

3. Michael Porter, *The Competitive Advantage of Nations* (New York: Free Press, 1990), p. 522.

4. Ibid., p. 375.

5. Brouthers, Werner, and Matulich, "The Influence of Triad Nations' Environments on Price-Quality Product Strategies and MNC Performance," p. 45.

6. Charles W. F. Baden-Fuller and John M. Stopford, "Globalization Frustrated: The Case of White Goods," *Strategic Management Journal* 12, no. 7 (1991): 495.

7. Frédérique Sachwald, ed., "European Integration and Competitiveness: Acquisitions and Alliances in Industry," quoted in Lance Eliot Brouthers and Timothy J. Wilkinson, "Is the EU Destroying European Competitiveness?" *Business Horizons*, July–August 2002, p. 39.

8. William Dietrich, *In the Shadow of the Rising Sun* (University Park, PA: Penn State University Press), pp. 116–117.

9. Porter, *The Competitive Advantage of Nations*, p. 404.

10. Kenichi Ohmae, "Getting Back to Strategy," *Harvard Business Review*, November–December 1988, p. 151.

11. Ritu Lohtia and Ramesh Subramaniam, "Structural Transformation of the Japanese Retail Distribution System," *Journal of Business and Industrial Marketing* 15, no. 5 (2000): 232.

12. Tohru Wako and Hiroshi Ohta, "Who Benefits from Corroding Keiretsu?" *Pacific Economic Review* 10, no 4 (2005): 539–556.

13. Masayoshi Maruyama, "Japanese Distribution Channels," *Japanese Economy* 32, no. 3 (2004): 27–48.

14. JETRO, "Retail Trends in Japan," 2007, available at http://www.jetro.go.jp/en/reports/market/pdf/2007_03_l.pdf.

15. U.S. Census Bureau, "Statistics of U.S. Businesses: 2004, U.S. Retail Trade," available at http://www.census.gov/epcd/susb/2004/us/US44.HTM.

16. Jack Kaikati, "Don't Crack the Japanese Distribution System-Just Circumvent It," *Columbia Journal of World Business* 28, no. 2 (1993): 34–45.

17. Information in this section and accompanying tables were drawn from the Environmental Protection Agency, "Municipal Solid Waste in

the United States: Facts and Figures," 2007, available at http://epa.gov/osw/nonhaz/municipal/pubs/msw07-rpt.pdf.

18. Phil Simmons, Nora Goldstein, Scott M. Kaufman, Nickolas J. Themelis, and James Thompson Jr., "The State of Garbage in America," *BioCycle* 47, no. 4 (2006): 4.

19. Elizabeth Royte, *Garbage Land: On the Secret Trail of Trash* (New York: Little, Brown, 2005).

20. Royte, *Garbage Land*, as quoted by Jennifer Weeks, *In Business* 27, no. 5 (2005): 24, available at http://209.85.173.132/search?q=cache:jcFDXdOtO8oJ:www.jgpress.com/inbusiness/archives/_free/000686.html+Streams+of+mixed+plastic+can+be+turned+into+only+one+other&cd=1&hl=en&ct=clnk&gl=us&client=firefox-a.

21. Ibid.

22. Charles Fishman, *The Wal-Mart Effect* (New York: Penguin Books, 2006), p. 178. On Chilean salmon, see Alexei Barrionuevo, "Facing Deadly Fish Virus, Chile Introduces Reforms," *New York Times*, September 4, 2008; and Jimmy Langman, "'Atlantic Salmon' a Fishy Tale: Chilean Industry Criticized for Pollution, Sneaky Labeling," *San Francisco Chronicle*, April 1, 2002.

23. James Fallows, "China's Silver Lining," *The Atlantic Monthly*, June 2008, available at http://www.theatlantic.com/doc/200806/pollution-in-china.

24. Joseph Kahn and Jim Yardley, "As China Roars, Pollution Reaches Deadly Extremes," *New York Times*, August 26, 2007; Mary-Anne Toy, "Pollution Facts Suppressed by China," *Sydney Morning Herald*, July 5, 2007; James Fallows, "China Makes, the World Takes," *The Atlantic Monthly*, July–August 2007.

25. A. T. Kearney, "New Concerns in an Uncertain World: The 2007 A. T. Kearney Foreign Direct Investment Confidence Index," 2007.

AFTERWORD

For many companies, the lure of partnering with a Mega-distributor is irresistible. Giants like Wal-Mart Stores and Home Depot can put products in front of hundreds of millions of customers—and potentially bring in huge gains in sales and market share.

But behind those high hopes may be a faulty premise that can lead to disaster. Whether out of naïveté, arrogance, or greed, innovative companies expect that the Megas will care about the success of their products and services as much as they do.

What companies forget, or ignore, is that the Mega's business model depends on mass marketing, low price, and volume. Naturally, the Megas use their tremendous leverage to dictate tough terms to manufacturers. They insist on ever-greater price reductions and force companies to redesign products and services to better suit their needs.

And, in the end, many companies discover that all the blood, sweat, tears, and money they have poured into their products and services has been wasted: Their hard-won creations have been turned into commodities with razor-thin profit margins.

This is particularly damaging for companies with innovative products. In the hands of a Mega, shelves are packed with competing products from multiple manufacturers. An innovative product loses its luster when it is surrounded by a slew of potential substitutes, many of which are cheap knockoffs. Numerous companies agree to make copies of their own brands for mass-market retailers. Compounding the problem, store clerks receive little or no training on the specifics of the products on display. Employees may know only where a product is located, not what makes it stand out. From this perspective, the outcomes for the innovator are not surprising: the abandonment of brand integrity, the acceleration of the innovation into a commodity, and the inevitable cost cuts that results from offshoring and outsourcing.

Having created the process and product, and invested time and money, why would companies turn the final stage of the operation over to a third party? Business leaders do it all the time. It is their choice and they must bear responsibility for what happens.

To avoid these outcomes, companies must control their own distribution. This may mean selling directly to customers online or through company-owned retail stores. Or, it may mean striking strong deals with distributors, and avoiding partners who will not agree to stringent terms.

Of course, avoiding the Megas may mean less volume, but the advantages of doing so are likely to make up for it. Companies that keep a tight rein on distribution have a greater ability to control pricing, customer service, and after-sales service. They can also build stronger, longer-lasting relationships with their customers. And that is what every company ultimately needs.

In 2008, Jack Weil, the "patriarch of Western clothing," died. According to an obituary published in *The Economist*, Weil was the inventor of the cowboy shirt. He was the one who put those snap fasteners on western wear, ensuring that cattlemen would not get snagged by cactus, sagebrush, or the horns of steers. Other adornments were added, including sawtooth flaps for pockets, a narrow fit to emphasize broad shoulders, and tight seams to show off the muscularity of the cowboy. Weil manufactured and sold his shirts through his Denver-based Rockmount Ranch Wear. The shirts were manufactured in the United States. The idea of outsourcing to China was inconceivable to him. The obituary in *The Economist* states the following:

> In his long, long life, Mr. Weil accumulated plenty of simple business sense. He knew J.C. Penney, and thought him smart. Levi-Strauss was a nice fellow, but got too big for his britches; Sam Walton, founder of Wal-Mart, was a "hillbilly SOB." Walton constantly harassed him to supply Wal-Mart with shirts, but Mr. Weil never wanted any customer to take more than 5% of his business. He felt he would lose control that way, and he considered discounters low-life in general. What mattered were two things, quality, and knowing the customer.[1]

It seems that Weil intuitively understood the dangers of the Distribution Trap. We can only hope that other innovators and entrepreneurs will similarly share in this insight.

NOTES

1. Obituary, "Jack Weil," *The Economist*, August 30, 2008.

ACKNOWLEDGMENTS

Together we would like to recognize Manseok Han, Donald L. Kaufman, and Terry Kelley of the Meridian Group; Fred Whyte and Anita Gambill of STIHL USA; and Dan Thomas, the STIHL expert at Billings Hardware, for the valuable time they gave us while we were writing this book.

Charles Baden-Fuller, the editor of *Long Range Planning*, and Dennis Organ, the former editor of *Business Horizons*, provided incredibly insightful comments on working papers related to this topic.

Great thanks are also owed to Michael Hopkins, editor-in-chief at *MIT Sloan Management Review*, and to Erin White and Rob Toth at the *Wall Street Journal*, for believing in this project from the beginning.

Finally, we will always be indebted to our editor, Jeff Olson, who continues to critique our work and show the confidence that allows us to take on even greater challenges as authors.

I am grateful to the team at The Taylor Institute for Direct Marketing at the University of Akron—Dale Lewison, Bill Hauser, Mike Kormushoff, and Steve Brubaker—for allowing me to be part of the finest program of its kind anywhere in the world. In addition, Karen Nelsen, Deborah Owens, Jim Barnett, Jim Emore, and Doug Hausknecht have each been so helpful as I made the transition from the business world to academe. Because of these folks, I have been able to find a new home. Go Zips!

My great friend Craig Vinkovich listened intently as I talked about this book for almost ten years. Dave Dealy, co-author and friend, is the finest conversationalist I know. The time spent with

Mark Koepsel was incredibly illuminating, especially on this subject but also on many others. Thanks to each of you for all of your steadfastness. I am eternally grateful to my wife, Jackie, and children, Paul Bryan and Alana.

—*Andrew R. Thomas*

I would like to thank Dean Gary Young and my colleagues at the College of Business at Montana State University–Billings for their ongoing support. I am also grateful to José Antonio Rosa, professor of marketing and sustainable business practices at the University of Wyoming, and Lance Eliot Brouthers, professor of management at Kennesaw State University, for their ongoing encouragement.

Thanks also to my sister-in-law, Nancy Van Maren, the toughest editor I have ever met, for her thoughts on an earlier draft. And to my wife Diane, who put up with the usual inconvenience imposed on spouses by book writers.

—*Timothy J. Wilkinson*

INDEX

ABOUT THE AUTHORS

ANDREW R. THOMAS is assistant professor of international business and associate director of the Taylor Institute for Direct Marketing at the University of Akron. A *New York Times* bestselling business writer, he is author, co-author, or editor of 16 books, including *Global Manifest Destiny, Managing by Accountability, Defining the Really Great Boss, Change or Die!* and *Direct Marketing in Action,* which was a finalist for the American Marketing Association's Berry Award for the Best Marketing Book of 2008. A successful global entrepreneur, Professor Thomas has traveled to and conducted business in more than 120 countries on all seven continents. He also serves on the visiting faculty of the International School of Management and Emmanuel University in Oradea, Romania.

Thomas is a noted authority on supply chain and transportation security. His books include *Supply Chain Security: International Practices and Innovations for Moving Goods Efficiently and Safely; Aviation Insecurity: The New Challenges of Air Travel; Air Rage: Crisis in the Skies; Aviation Security Management* (3 vols.); and *The Handbook of Supply Chain Security.* Thomas is founding-editor-in-chief of the *Journal of Transportation Security.* He is a regularly featured media analyst for MSNBC, CNN, BBC, and Fox News.

TIMOTHY J. WILKINSON is associate professor of marketing at Montana State University Billings. Before returning to the Rocky Mountains region, he taught for eight years at the University of Akron, where he served as the associate director of the Institute for Global Business. He has taught a wide variety of business courses to undergraduates and MBA students. In addition, he has lectured in the doctoral programs at the University of Texas at El Paso and Kennesaw State University. A frequent visitor to Romania, Wilkinson has delivered lectures at the Academy of Economic Studies, Vasile Goldia West University, and Emmanuel University.

Professor Wilkinson is a noted expert in the area of exports and export promotion. His academic papers include publications in *Long Range Planning*, the *Journal of Business Research*, the *Journal of International Business Studies*, *International Business Review*, and the *Journal of Small Business Research*.

ANDREW R. THOMAS'S and TIMOTHY J. WILKINSON'S cutting-edge research on sales and distribution strategy has appeared in the *Wall Street Journal*, *MIT Sloan Management Review*, and *Business Horizons*, as well as in the four-volume set *Marketing in the 21st Century*. For more on the issues raised in this book, go to http://www.distributiontrap.com.